Glenn Alterman is the author of *STREET TALK (CHARACTER MONOLOGUES FOR ACTORS)*, a featured selection in Doubledays Fireside Theater Book Club, where it recently went into it's second printing. His monologue plays (series of monologues) include: *Kiss Me When it's Over* (commissioned by E. Weissman Productions) starred Andre De Shields (La Mama); *Tourists of the Mindfield*, a semi finalist in the L. Arnold Weissberger Playwriting Competition at New Dramatists in New York; *Dirty Prayers*, commissioned by Sydelle Marshall Productions; and *God in Bed*, which premiered at the West Bank Cafe Downstairs Theater Bar in New York. The first production of *Street Talk* (monologues from the book), premiered at the West Coast Ensemble in Hollywood, California. *Heartstrings*, (commissioned by the Design Industries Foundation For Aids) received a 30 city National Tour with a cast of 35 including Michelle Pfeiffer, Ron Silver, Christopher Reeve, Susan Sarandon, Marlo Thomas, and Sandy Duncan. His first "dialogue" play, *Goin' Round on Rock Solid Ground*, was a finalist at The Actors Theater of Louisville (out of 2500 plays), and received workshop productions at the Circle Rep Lab and West Bank Cafe Downstairs Theater Bar. His next play, *Spilt Milk* recently received a workshop production at the West Bank Cafe Downstairs Theater Bar. A production of *STREET TALK/UPTOWN* (monologues from the books) will premiere at The Fountainhead Theater in Los Angeles in the fall of 1992.

NOBODY'S FLOOD, Mr. Altermans latest play, will have a workshop production at the West Bank Cafe Downstairs Theater Bar, also in the fall of 1992.

MONOLOGUES
The Best Women's Stage Monologues of 1992
The Best Men's Stage Monologues of 1991
The Best Men's Stage Monologues of 1990
The Best Women's Stage Monologues of 1992
The Best Women's Stage Monologues of 1991
The Best Women's Stage Monologues of 1990
Street Talk: Character Monologues for Actors
One Hundred Men's Stage Monologues from the 1980's
One Hundred Women's Stage Monologues from the 1980's
The Great Monologues from the Humana Festival
The Great Monologues from the EST Marathon
Monologues from Contemporary Literature: Volume I
Monologues from Classic Plays

YOUNG ACTORS
Great Scenes for Young Actors from the Stage
Great Monologues for Young Actors
New Plays from A.C.T.'s Young Conservatory
Scenes and Monologues for Very Young Actors

ADVANCED ACTORS
The Best Stage Scenes for Women from the 1980's
The Best Stage Scenes for Men from the 1980's
The Best Stage Scenes of 1992
The Actor's Chekhov

PLAYS FOR ACTORS
The Best Plays of 1992 by Women Playwrights
Seventeen Short Plays by Romulus Linney

If you require pre-publication information about upcoming Smith and Kraus monologues collections, scene collections, play anthologies, advanced acting books, and books for young actors, you may receive our semi-annual catalogue, free of charge, by sending your name and address to Smith and Kraus Catalogue, P.O. Box 10, Newbury, VT 05051.

UPTOWN

Original monologues
by Glenn Alterman

SK
A Smith and Kraus Book

A Smith and Kraus Book
Published by Smith and Kraus, Inc.

Copyright © 1992 by Smith and Kraus, Inc.
All rights reserved

Manufactured in the United States of America

First Edition: December 1992
8 7 6 5 4 3 2 1

Library of Congress Cataloging-in-Publication Data

Alterman, Glenn, 1946 -
    Uptown: character monologues for actors / by Glenn Alterman.
        P. cm. -- (The Monologue audition series)
    Includes bibliographical references.
    ISBN 1-880399-08-3 : $8.95
    1. Acting--Auditions. 2. Monologues. I. Title. II. Series.
Pn2080.A45 1993
812'.54--dc20   92-37750
                                             CIP

Smith and Kraus, Inc.
One Main Street, PO Box 127, Lyme, NH 03768
(603) 795-4331

iv

ACKNOWLEDGMENTS

The playwright wishes to thank the following: Greg Jackson, Gloria Slofkiss, Bonnie Elmowitz, The West Bank Cafe Downstairs Theater Bar, Rowen Joseph, Rand Forrester, Steve Olson, L.B.Williams, La Mama, The West Coast Ensemble, The Fountainhead Theater (Andrew Shaefer), American Renaissance Theater, Sydelle Marshall, Catherine Wolf, Herb Rubens, Bob Ari, Marilyn Chris, Mary Harden- The Brett Adams Agency, Elowyn Castle, Ernie Barbarash, Daniel Dassin, Kenny Kramer and Susan Noss, Circle Rep Lab, and all the producers, directors and actors that gave their time, energy, and creativity.

CONTENTS
MEN

CONTENTS

WOMEN

CONTENTS

x

Finding the perfect monologue for an audition or a performance is always a problem for the actor. The goal is to find a solo piece where the character has an emotional range, comes to a realization or understanding, has strength and vulnerability and is changed in some way by the end. A hard bill to fill especially when you add to this the need to find a monologue that is unique and new to the auditor or audience.

What I most enjoy seeing in a monologue is its ability to carry you on an emotional journey. Whether the character portrayed evokes laughter, warmth or bitterness the journey must be intriguing. All the characters in Glenn Alterman's UPTOWN have this ability.

My introduction to Alterman's work was with STREET TALK — a book of monologues. They were brought to me in manuscript form by Sharon Lee Connors, who subsequently produced and was one of the directors of the West Coast premiere of STREET TALK. What was so involving about his work was Alterman's introspection into the soul of his characters. To quote Alterman, his monologues gave the actor "the dirt" to really immerse themselves in that seedy, bizarre or painful life his characters inhabit but with added humor to soften the edges and allow some hope. The West Coast Ensemble had the privilege of premiering ten of the monologues from STREET TALK. The audience's response to an evening of solo performances was amazing and the sale of Alterman's monologue book surpassed the overwhelming feedback from our humble evening of monologues. Alterman's work is still remembered and praised here at the West Coast Ensemble.

With UPTOWN Alterman again gives life to those corners of the city we would never know existed. He takes us from the street to the upper west side. He lets us hear the whispered dreams of Tonya and her tuck away wings, we are allowed to be in the esteemed

xi

company of Dora — a wealthy, chic shoplifter and we feel the electric passion between Sadie and her rabbi over a bagel. Bizarre? Yes. Enticing? Yes. In UPTOWN, Glenn Alterman continues to help actors in their search for the perfect monologue .

Les Hanson
Artistic Director
West Coast Ensemble
Hollywood, California

Naturally, I was more than thrilled by the enthusiastic success of STREET TALK, my first book. The letters and phone calls I've received have been very encouraging as well as informative. The feedback from actors, directors, and casting directors have all made a valuable contribution in the writing of UPTOWN.

One thing I realized was that both actors and casting directors are basically looking for the same thing in a monologue. That is, interesting, compelling characters telling a good story; a good yarn.

While actors are looking for material that is emotionally gripping and involving, casting directors want (aside from a good performance) stories that interest and entertain.

In Uptown, I've tried to create characters that need to speak; feel compelled too. It's that need, I believe, that makes these characters vibrant and alive- more engaging.

There are more variety of character types in this book. More colors to play. Different moods. And judging by the initial response we had at the readings, I feel that by and large this crop of monologues will satisfy even the most hard to please actor.

Again, I wish to thank you for all your encouragement and comments. And wish you the best of luck.

Glenn Alterman
New York City
August, 1992

dedicated to
Sadie Rosenthal
and
John Dickson Fisher

UPTOWN

Original monologues
by Glenn Alterman

SK
A Smith and Kraus Book

30'-50's - an airline waiting area at the Miami Beach Airport. Marvin is a high strung, somewhat volatile man who has just missed his plane. Here he pours out his rage to an innocent fellow traveler who just happens to be seated in the waiting area.

(As Marvin arrives things are falling off of him. He is in a total frenzy. His luggage is half opened. In one hand he carries the broken luggage carrier. The luggage carrier cords are dangling from his pockets. Under his arms are several frayed newspapers. In the other hand he carries a crushed cup of soda with a bent strawer. This is not a happy man!)

Sons a bitches! God damn Eagle Air! They promised! I knew I shouldn't a listened! I knew it! But they promised! Gave me their word! An' you depend on 'em, ya know?! Give 'em ya money, ya life, ya credit cards! Say they'll get'cha there on time. BULLSHIT! BULL-SHIT!! Told me about their ninety-five per cent on time arrivals. Ninety-five per cent! Well guess who got the other five?! GUESS! (doesn't give him a chance)

Said I'd have no problem. That's what he said. Plane-Plane. Not to worry. FORTY-FIVE MINUTES LATE! FORTY-FIVE!! An' then... THEN the pilot first starts taxiing all over the place. Looking for a parking spot or something. Took us on a sightseeing tour! Musta seen every inch of the Miami Airport. Forty minutes more! Till finally we stopped, thank God! Stewardess gives us the plastic good byes, we're like horses at the gate- and the door to the plane gets stuck. Jammed! They hadda get a mechanic from outside. Kept us there 'nother half hour! An' while standing there waiting for the mechanic to get the door opened, sweating, I look out the window and what do I see? My plane, Key West Airlines, the twelve o'five taking off. On time! Right before my eyes. Couldn't fuckin' believe it! My dream of sitting at a cool pool drinking margaritta's with fresh lime- gone. Being able to relax, let myself go- gone! And I stood there, just stood there, helpless, crammed together with all the others. And all I could think was FUCK THE FRIENDLY SKIES!! It's 'cause of them. They did it- Eagle Air! It's because of them- there goes my vacation!!!

30's-50's - The Limbo Lounge, a piano bar. The limbo Lounge is a dream filled, fantasy, piano bar. Here, Mr. Piano Player, your host, welcomes you to this magical place.

(Warmly, big smile, very friendly)
Well, how ya doin' tanight, huh? Gooood!
Nice... Nice ta see ya again.
Lookin' good.
    You lose weight? You look great!
Somethin' ya wanna hear?
    C'mon, c'mere.
        Favorite song you'd like...
    Pull up a chair... Yeah!
An' welcome.
    Welcome to your dreams sir.
An' dreams...
            dreams a' nothin' more n' wishes, y'see?
                An' me,
                    I can make 'em all come true.
Yeah!
    S'easy. Nothin' to it.
    Jus' my fingers floatin' down the iv'ries.
    Old melodies,
        Show tunes,
            an' the "magic" in the room.
Yeeeeeaaaahhhh!
(sleazy) 'Cause ahm a pimp at the piano,
        the song's the whore.
            Put a buck in the bowl
                if ya want-
                    put more.
Pure fantasy here— Yeah!
Big smiles— see, everyone's singin'.
    S'the nightly routine.
    In ya walk,
    have a seat,
        in ya own private dream.
(soft and abrupt) But-please-don't-shoot-the-piano-player

(delicately, almost a beg) It's fatal... An' I'm fragile.
(Suddenly big) But like Superman
    I'm faster than a plane.
    I can unlock the prison,
        an' let out ya pain.
(To a lady in the room) An' maybe you're in luck miss.
    Ya might meet a friend.
    Put a buck in the bowl,
        an' I'll play it again.
            That song ya loved.
                Remember?
Rita sang it-
    that torchy tune.
        I'll conjure up the moment,
        we'll go back to the forties,
        when men were men,
        an' girls were just
            "naughty".
When it was chic
    to go to clubs in minks,
        smokin' long cigarettes,
            while sippin' ya drinks.
In piano bars— just like ours.
    When Judy, Marlene, an' Betty were stars.
    Let me take you there— yeah!
        With a song-sung-blue.
        How's about a tune- from Follies?
        Or if ya like- I'll play somethin' new.
I'll excite you,
I invite you,
Do some old tricks
    that are new.
    Put a buck in the bowl,
        let the music get to you.
            Let it loosen,
                an' lighten.
                    Let go of your day.
It's the magic in the moment that'll make ya wanna stay.
S'the spell.

I weave
  only here
    every night.
But... please
  don't shoot me— if I don't get it just right.
These are,
  after all,
    just dreams.
An' things in here ain't what they seem.
  WE IN A PIANO BAR, BABY! !
  Where nostalgia and sentiment are never dead.
      Ya gotta open ya heart,
        an' take off your head.
An' after a while,
  after a while,
  I think you'll see,
      maybe even agree...
        That I need you like you need me!
An' everything costs, baby.
Ain't nothin' for free.
  Please...
      put a buck in the bowl,
        an' come with me
            to Never Never Land.
    With the boys in the band,
        an' the ladies always waiting.
  'Cause everyone here is masquerading
        in a memory
At our piano bar,
    where no one's an "extra"
        everyone's a "star"!
Come sit inside,
  s'just me and you.
    We'll sing some songs
        you'll see how dreams
          really do
            really...
                come true.

50'-70's A very chic cocktail party in a gallery in Soho. T.S., a very sophisticated older gentleman, has always been a prominent fixture in the art world. He's always invited to the most "in" parties, knows the most up and coming artists, and is always seen with the "right" people. Here, while walking with a new "protege", showing him around, he admits his one secret yearning.

(while walking. Very "grand")
Look at her. See.
　Her claim to fame,
　　her claim to fame
　　　was that she photographed John Lennon
　　　　two hours before he died.
　　　　　There's a book.
　　　　　Lots of money.
　　　　　　Come. (They continue walking)
Notice (They stop)
　everyone here in trendy black.
　　But how many know the host...
　　　　　I wonder.
　　　　　　Very few,
　　　　　　　I'm sure.
Come. (they continue walking)
　He... He's a haberdasher,
　　　　thinks he's a couturier.
She... has fallen
　　obviously.
　　　　Even the lifts don't help anymore.
And you,
　you my young friend,
　　　you're an odd one.
　　You tell me,
　　　　you say you know
　　　　　where there is art in Soho.
　Lord knows I've looked
　　through the surface and the glitz.

But I can't seem to find it...
             anywhere .
                      Where's it happening?
                      Tell me!
How far below Canal Street must I go?
The river is only so deep.
                      And the truth reflects, yes?
                      Then show me- please!
(Pause)
      Would you care for another canape?
(then)
      I don't know if you can answer.
      I don't know if I can hear.
          Look
              jade
                  everywhere.
But...
      the truth
          is the truth
              is the truth, right?
I mean,
      it's not the Holy Grail,
          (looking around) and we aren't La Dolce Vita.
But I must admit
      my personal search
          is quietly consistent.
                      A constant,
                          from party,
                              to party,
                                  to galas,
                                      to openings.
When I go out,
      I'm always looking.
      Always.
(pause)
          You are a hope for me, you know.
              I still do dream
                  believe it or not.
                      And I do understand your reticence...

6

even your misbelieving.

But your eyes...

show such knowing.

Do you?

DO YOU?!

Tell me

please!

Where?

Have I missed it?

Must I beg?!

Is there

truth

around

somewhere?

Please,

tell me my wise young friend.

Do you know?

Is there art

in Soho?

30's-40's - sitting at the kitchen table. Mickey, Barrys brother has committed suicide because he knew he was dying of Aids. Here Barry tells his parents about the last time he saw his brother.

The reason I came here that night was because Mickey needed me; needed my help. We'd been talking, well arguing about it for a long time- months. But he was determined. And ma, you knew Mickey, once he made his mind up on something, that was it. But still, I came here to try and talk him out of it. One last plea. But he wouldn't listen. Wanted one thing and one thing only, for us to go down to the ocean like we used to. Said he couldn't make it there himself, was too weak. Was going to be his last hurrah, he said. We argued, he threatened, I yelled. Till finally, as usual, I gave in. I gave in 'cause... well, I knew if I didn't he'd get there by himself. Crawl if he had too. I just let him have some dignity.

Alright, so we went. I took him, and we sat on the beach. Had like a little party. Talked about everything. Growing up, old times, I don't know. Then he got quiet. Like all of a sudden. Very quiet. We sat there on the beach in the dark, listening to the ocean. Just sat there. Then he drank some vodka, took the pills, and got up. He looked at me, and said, "I love you Barry." Gave me a big hug, then said, "Good bye", and went down to the water. Just like that. I watched him, then I stood up, went down to the water, and watched him swim out until I couldn't see him anymore. Till he just like disappeared. I stood there for I don't know how long. Just stood there. Numb. Then I went back to the airport, and waited for Brenda.

Any age- a small town. While going out for the morning paper, Gregory sees something horrible written across the front of his house. The shock, and how he deals with it is what this monologue is about.

You don't expect it. Not here. Not... This is a small town. We all know each other. Our families have grown up here. I had... I think what upset me the most was not just that they chose my house, but that they did it while I was inside, asleep. Sleeping. Unable...

When I got up this morning, went out for the paper, when I turned around and saw it- the writing all over the front of the house. The black paint... Was that moment, the shock, I'll never forget. Standing there in my bathrobe-numb. All I could think was, My God. My God, who hates so much? Who has so much hate in them?

I just stood there. Didn't know what to do. The feeling... I couldn't move. But then, finally I went back in. Filled a bucket with warm water, some cleaner. Got some steel pads, and went back out. Started to scrub. Started scrubbing. Could feel the steel pads going into my fingers. Saw the paint getting all over my white robe. Kept scrubbing! Harder! Hard as I could! Till I could see the letters disappearing. Pushing! Rubbing against the wood! Against their words! Hard as I could! Till I could feel, till I felt as much hate, rage as they. And I kept scrubbing. Scrubbing! Till there wasn't a word or a letter left. Nothing. Till it was the way it use to be, before. Then I turned around, and looked. I wanted to see if they were watching. If they knew. But nobody was there. So I threw the steel pads into the bucket and went back in. Closed the door, washed my hands, changed clothes, and looked out the window. No one. No one. But I'll wait. I'll stay here and wait for them. Yes I will. No matter how long. No matter how long it takes.

20's-40's — a black rally headquarters. Here, Raheem, a black militant, attempts to convince another black man to join a looting group

(passionately, with fervor)

S'a fuckin' feelin' like flyin' man! Lettin' loose! Outta the bag! Be brothers everywhere, all around. Streets like liquid-free flowin'. A black river a brothers unified! Nights ours man- we own it! Takin' back for all brothers-everywhere! We be racin' through them streets, fists raised-power signin'! Burnin' cars! Settin' fires! Sayin', "Honkeys, we here! We here mother fuckers! Takin' over. Takin' back what shoulda been. Taken back what's ours!

Grabbin! Lootin'! Stealin' from a shelf! Takin' man, yeah. Takin' back the night for them brothers a long ago. For them, man. That's why. S'what it's all about! For him-Mr. Black Somebody. Ole Mr. Black Somebody, who was kicked down, spit on, an' called Nigger all his life. For him, man. Him, who never could. But we can!

An' for his ole woman, who hadda lay down with Massuh Honkey behind closed doors. Hadda make that massuh happy. Do what he want. Then go out an' wash his dirty laundry to make him feel clean. For her man, we gonna open them doors- wide! Burglar alarms gonna trumpet our arrival! Breakin' glass s'gonna shatter, sayin' "We here! We here mother fuckers! An' the plantations closed! Pick your own fuckin' cotton! "

That's what goin' out tonight means. What it spells to 'em. Don'chu see? You gotta come! You gotta! Cause if you don't man, you be Uncle Tommin' your way back, an' never get into Kunti Kinti's backyard. Be somebodys kiss my white ass slave; changin tires at some honkey gas station for less'n minimum wage. An you don't want that man. We passed that shit on the road a long time ago. Way back in the sixties.

Come on man, come with us. Help us take back the night for all them brothers. It's the right thing man. Come!

30's-50's - Anywhere. Merv decided to sneak away; escape from his responsibilities by going to a movie. Here he tells about the life and death experience he had while watching the movie, Terminator Two.

It seemed almost sinful. I don't know, maybe it's the dark or the cool. Or maybe it's knowing I'm playing hookey from work. But there's something delightfully bad about sneaking off to a movie on a hot, summer, weekday afternoon. But I felt I needed to. So I just did. Bought my ticket, went inside. Entered the cool, ready to escape.

Got a big bag of buttered popcorn and a large coke. Found a seat and relaxed. Couldn't help but noticing the theater's almost empty. Good. Got myself an almost private screening. Loosened my tie, took off my jacket. Got comfy, cozy, and relaxed. Lights started coming down, slowly. This is going to be good! Curtain goes up- yes! Take me away! Don't want to think about clients, accounts, my family, anything. Just want to be taken away - movie magic. Arnold Schwartzenegger- Terminator Two. Let's go Arnie- yeah! Dolby sound waking me up, pulling me in. Opening credits. This is going to be good! Gobble up some popcorn, take a swig of my coke. Let's go Arnie! I'm right with you buddy. Closer than your shadow, under your skin. Our adventure- together!

Take a quick swig of popcorn, gobble up some coke. Gobble, but then... then... Hey! Wait! What...? It's stuck! Something... The popcorns stuck in my throat! Can't...! Can't... breathe. S'caught!

Look around. Other seats are empty. No one! Can't breathe!! Somebody! My life starts flashing by like in a movie- but hey, wait, I'm in a movie! This is a movie theater! CAN'T BREATHE!! Start grabbing at my throat, ripping at my shirt! Drop the popcorn, the coke. Hear them splatter on the floor, miles away. Look up to the screen, to Arnold. As if... Arnie can't help! Can't breathe!!

Then suddenly I realize- I'm gonna die! Die!

Then a light. Just like they say. A bright light in the

distance. A bright light shining. Then a voice- "Mister! Mister, you okay?!" I'm pulled up out of my seat. Yanked up like a rag doll. A push to my chest! A push to my stomach! A slap on the back! What?! What's happening? Help! Then... then it pops outa piece of popcorn. I gasp for air. Breathe! Breath!

Again the voice- "You okay?! Want me to get someone?" "What?! No! No... Thank you! Thank... I'm fine!

The light- a flashlight. My savior, my hero- the usher. A kid a few years older than my son. A kid!

"Thank you! Thank you so much!"

Catch my breath. A small crowd has gathered. Two or three people appear from nowhere. Where were they when...?

"I'm fine, really. You can all... I'm okay. Thank you, really!"

Slowly, they go back to wherever. The usher pats me on the back. "Now you take care of yourself mister. Don't eat so fast." He turns his flashlight off, leaves. I am so embarrassed! Finally I settle back in my seat and just breathe. Take deep breaths for a minute or two. Breathe. What was that about? Look up at the screen. At Arnie. Where were you?! Sit up in my seat. My God, talk of an adventure! Relax. Just wanted a little escape, that's all. Just... Jesus! Breathe. Talk of an adventure!

30's-50's - Anywhere. Douglas, a bald man, talks about his obsession with being bald, and how he finally resolved it.

It was a sign. A Xeroxed sheet. A piece of paper on a bulletin board. Right outside the A&P. I'd just come from shopping and I noticed it. In big, bold print the sign said, "MUST BE SEEN! UNBELIEVABLE! THE MOST GENUINE HAIR PIECES **EVER! EVER!**" I thought, well anyone who has the nerve to write the word "ever" twice and then underline it, well maybe, perhaps, it might be...? Who knows? Maybe a chance. A chance! A possibility. And for those of us who have suffered; experienced the deep feelings of inadequacy, cosmetic deficiency. For those of us who have tried every tincture, tonic, ointment, and cream, and were always left frustrated. For those of us who are bald, and have learned that only concealment and cover up are the only real solution. For us- me, this sign outside the A&P, promising miraculous hair was like a pot of gold at the end of yet another rainbow. A hope! So I tore off a tab, went home, and called.

A very old voice at the other end said, "Yes", he possessed these magic toupees. Swore that if I wore one, just tried it on, he guaranteed I'd never want to take it off again- ever!

"When could I see one?", I asked. Told me he'd be right over. I hung up. And while waiting... while waiting the anticipation began to drive me mad. I began pacing-feverishly! Dreams- old hopes, rekindled. Images flashed through my mind. Dreams of long, lush, thick hair. The possibility! My plate would be full; my head finally covered.

The doorbell rang. And in walked this tiny, toothless, decrepit old man wearing an unpressed suit. He had thick, gray, greasy, long hair. In his frail hands he carried a big, brown box. After very quick hello's, I asked, "Is this...? Are they...?" He said, "Yes, they're in there."

Slowly I opened the box, searched through the layers of tissue paper until I found them. An assortment- all colors. And yes they were- unbelievable! They looked, felt, even smelled- smelled real! It was astonishing! Frantically I searched for one similar to my natural color. I found one my exact shade, placed it on my head. A sound like a suction. It fit- like a glove. I ran to the mirror. Stood there. Stared. It was... unbelievable. Incredible! I turned around, checked it from every angle. I'd never seen anything like it. Never! It was even better... better than my own hair ever was! Ever! So... after years and years of searching, this was it. The pot of gold. The end of the journey. Journeys end. My search was over! I now... felt complete. An acceptable member of the human race. Younger, more attractive, virile,- significant! I had my hair.

I turned to the old man... but he was gone! I wanted to thank him. Pay him... but he'd left. The door was still open. Strange. I mean no bill, no card, no charge. Of course. Of course, I finally realized, he was a great humanitarian. This was a gift. For a lifetime of suffering. God bless him!

I ran back to the mirror. Stared, studied myself, from every angle. Astounding! It was incredible. I've never looked so well. Pulled up a chair, kept turning, peeking over my shoulder, like this. (he demonstrates) Then a quick look. Another, and another. Hour after hour, just staring. Smiling at myself. Hours! Hours! Until I fell asleep, sitting there.

When I woke up this morning, before my first breath, I looked- to be sure. (He touches his bald head) To be certain that I wasn't dreaming. So you can just imagine how happy I was... to see myself looking... (he stops, smiles, touches his head again) Tell the truth. If I hadn't told you, you'd never have known, right? (He continues touching his scalp) If you'd passed me, say at a restaurant, or in an elevator, you'd never know. How could you? It's remarkable, isn't it? I think part of it are these curls here. They add... something, don't you think? Maybe it's the way they fall. So naturally. (He continues touching his scalp, caressing his "hair", feverishly) And the smell! You should smell my hair. Smells just like after a nice shampoo. I mean really, isn't it... isn't it... magnificent?! Notice how full! How lush it is! (He continues touching his "hair" in wild abandon, as the lights come down) It's the thickness, I think. The incredible texture! The bounce. The. . .

14

Early 20's- Arnold's friend Harry's apartment.
Arnold, a young, aspiring, stand up comic has
finally booked his first gig. Here he excitedly
tells his teacher and mentor what has
happened.

(full of life, high charged, enthusiastic)

I took 'em for the ride Harry! Was just like you said. I
was glide-flyin' through the piece, ridin' solo, and I hit every
peak! Held 'em captive, an' they never missed a beat! Never
Harry, never!

Yeah sure, I know s'just a dumpy club in Brooklyn, an'
he's not the King of England, but I had em! I had em!

So afta' ahm through, there's another beat, an' then a
WALL A LAUGHTER! They loved me! You get it? I was a
hit! On top!

An' they're laughin', sayin', "Terrific! Terrific! Who
writes ya stuff?"

An' I turned, took my time, said real slow, "I do. Me.
My. Mine. I write my own."

There's a gasp! The room shook! They were shocked!

An' I knew then, jus' like you been tellin' me since day
one- I got it! I got it! An' alls I gotta do is "put it out! Put it
out!"

Alright, so I'm up there, fermentin' in the moment.
Should I stay? Should I go? What?!

Then he says, "Ahm gonna book ya two weeks straight,
top scale." An' I said, "Yeah, sure." But makin' like I deserve
it, y'know? Then I flew back here on the subway!

Harry... Harry this is the greatest day a my life! The
dream, remember?! Right?!

(Calmer) Look, I don't wanna get sappy with ya, but jus'
thanks.. Thanks... for always bein' there... in my corner.
Means a lot

Well... I better get goin'. Gotta do some more writin'-for
my "public". Gotta lot to say. Dreams don't die, right?!

Right, Harry?! YEAH! Catch ya later, man.

60's-70's the bedroom. Edna, Murrays wife has just revealed to Murray a secret she's held on to for over forty years. She's told him that her sister Martha accused Murray of trying to force himself on her one day when they were alone in a blueberry field. **Murray becomes furious when he hears what Martha accused him of. Here, he tells Edna his side of the story.**

I'll tell you what happened. An' I want you to listen good! 'Cause I got nothin' to be ashamed of. Nothin' to hide. S'your sister Martha...! Okay, okay, so we went to the woods. When we got there Martha wasn't in the mood to do no pickin'. No, she's just lyin' there in the grass; longin' around, watchin' me do all the work. An' pretty soon, your Martha starts talkin' 'bout how she knew her Herbie was cheatin' on her. Was no secret. An' how she's still a young woman. How she still got her looks. An' how what's good for the goose is good for the gander. An' I knew what she meant. Knew exactly! But I ignored her. Didn't pay it no mind. Just kept pickin' blueberries. But she keeps lookin' over at me, ya sister. Smilin'. Then I notice... I noticed ya sisters skirt was way up her legs. She's lyin' there, playin' with the grass, lookin' up at me. An' I couldn't help but notice that she didn't have no underwear on. An' she's sayin, "Come on, come over here Murray. Come lie down with me." But when I didn't come, she come over to me. Start rubbin' against me, like massagin' my legs. Rubbin em'. Workin' her hands up. Till finally, I grab her hands an' said, "Look you, ahm ya sisters husband! Have you forgotten?! Have some respect!"

She jus' looked at me. Didn't say a word. Then I threw her hands down an said, "Go find yourself another alley to crawl in!"

Edna, everybody knew about your sister. You think I was the only one?! The first?! Right up until Herbie died, believe me, she fooled around plenty. Lots a guys! But never with me. Never!

An' then... then, she spit at me, your sister. So I slapped her face- hard! I did the slappin' that day, not her!

I was so angry I wanted to kill her.

Anyway... that's when she went running back to the bungalow, told you that cockamamie story a hers. And you believed her. Believed her all these years.

Any age- anywhere. Reggie makes out very well in bars. Both he and "the jazz man" have a seductive technique that never fails.

(laid back, jazzy)
   S'one thing I've learned pal
      in every bar I've been.
         S'always a jazz man there
            helpin ya out.
         Playin' the blues.
         His saxy-phone burnin',
            the music sayin':
      "Come on down.
      Come on down.
      Bedroom's in the bar if ya jus' look around."
So I do,
    as he plays.
Then find me a seat.
      An' put out a line
         to catch me a woman
            with some sweet talk
               an' bourbon.
            As we red-tongue-tango,
              till we're both smooth sailin' to hell.
(getting excited) We start to mambo!
                  Cha-cha!
                    Fling it around!
                      Push it together,
                        while takin' it down!
        I want to jump on the bar,
           rip off our clothes,
             an' say,
                NOW BABY! NOW BABY! NOW!
(more calm) But. . .
      hold back,
        stay cool,
          be calm.
            Listen to the music.

As my cigarettes drippin',
an the bar's gettin' warmer.
His melody persistin' for hours.
Till there's no one left
but us.
An' the jazz man.
Drivin' his music.
Smilin'
from a shelf.
Wavin' us on.
Time to go.
You never say good bye to a jazz man- no.
'Cause as you leave,
s'one last wink.
Ya smile
as you're takin' her home.
Then off you go-
See ya later, daddy-o.
Yeah Jazz Man. . .
till next time

30's-40's - Anywhere. Here Jim, a street person, talks about how his life changed after the night he fought with his two angel friends.

Was like a streetlight serenade
  given by my two angel friends,
    who I like to kid an' call
         Heckel an' Jeckel.
      'Cause they're always tootin' their damn trumpets
        like them cartoon magpies.
And so it started annoyin' me-
  listenin' to 'em,
    sittin' there,
      hangin out on the streets.
    Finally I said,
      "Look you two, cut it out!
         Them trumpets are drivin' me mad.
Well, you gotta know them- Heck an' Jeck,
  They're a fun-lovin' pair.
    Mischievous,
        always tryin' to get me to laugh.
        Fluffin' their wings,
          bouncin' about,
            distortin' my vision on things.
Well, outta all this,
    a squabble erupts- yeah!
         'Cause I wanna watch.
          But they wanna play.
    S'a conflict a interests.
    An' I want my way!
Well, shit in hell,
So do they! So do they!
  An it's trouble!
    S'heaven versus earth- with trumpets blowin'.
I said,
    "Look you two. Cut it out!
      Ya overstepped your line!
Well Heckel looks at Jeckel,
  two of 'em look real pissed.

Then Heckel says to Jeckel,
    "Get 'em!
"Get 'em!", he said.
 Just like that.
   Couldn't believe it- WAR!
Next thing,
 fists hit wings- we started to fight.
    Roll on the ground,
      in the middle of the night.
Ya gotta understand,
   we were friends.
    Always were
     Now there was bloodshed.
Right then and there,
  s'like my belief in the heavenly went.
    Couldn't see the difference between heaven
     an' hell.
   Just 'cause Heckel said to Jeckel,
      "Get em!"

An' they were angels. Angels!
 Pure little puffs.
  Good.
   God sent.
    The best!
But after they turned.
 After we fought
  was like hope an' trust
   flew out a window.
    Goodness disappeared.
Well,
 long story short,
  they won the fight.
Disappeared,
  flew off,
   somewhere in the night.
I sat on the curb,
  like in a stupor
   tryin' to figure out-
    "What was that about?!"

An' more important,
   where was God?
      Didn't he see?
         Where the hell was he?
            In bed, sleeping?
His angels had turned-
     An now there was a crack
       in the pavement.
So I sat there
     watchin' people pass.
       Sat,
          knowin' it was different.
Darkness had fallen.
The night had come.
   An' things looked different
       in the city.

60's- 80's - Anywhere. While sitting with his grandson, Morris remembers the good old days when he was a young man in Miami.

I wanna go back... to Miami, yeah. An' lie on that beach there. An lay in the sun, an' watch... the flamingoes play. There's coconuts, an' palm trees, an alligators in the everglades. But just layin' on that beach... watchin' the ocean, feelin' the sun, I can relax... an' forget things.

I hear they... they speak Spanish now on Collins Avenue. That there's a lot a Cubans. S'become a cocaine capital, but shit, who cares. Not me, nah. 'Cause I remember the old days, yeah. When everyone went over to Wolfies for pastrami. An' we wore white-white in the sun then. Everything was white. White suits, white shoes, white ties. An' me, I was always drivin' a white car, an' hadda dark tan. Yeah! You'd catch me cruisin' down Collins with the top down. Smellin good of lilac cologne or Old Spice. Always winkin' at some hot dish on a corner in a two piece an' heels. An' sonny, let me tell ya, in them days they were all blondes with long, long legs. An' they always smiled back at a good lookin' man with a tan in a convertible. Yeah.

Later on, when the sun went down, we'd go for a little ride somewhere. Then a rhumba or a cha-cha at some tiny cocktail lounge; out of the way, off a the beach. Candle lit, sunburned skin. Our hands touchin' while sipppin' our tall, cool drinks. Makin' eyes an' feelin' sexy all over. Yeah. Yes sir. Yes sir, I remember.

An' memories... memories are like little jewels, sonny. Gotta hold on to 'em. 'Cause... they wash away, an' then... then your old.

Sometimes... sometimes when I'm shavin', I look in the mirror an' think, "Who's that old man? Who's that? Not me. No." No, inside a me's a young man in a white car, winkin'; waitin' to get back to Miami. 'Cause I know kid, like for sure, that it's gonna be just the same as when I left. Alright, maybe the hotels got a little bigger, that's all. Yeah.

An' ahl have a truckload a blondes sittin' all around me, just like I usta. And we'll be laughin' in my long white car; as we're drivin' out, drivin' out inta the sun!

20's-30's - backstage at a huge sports arena. Here, Johnny Star, a mega rock and roll star, tells what it's like every time he goes out on the stage to perform.

(Wild, explosive energy)

I <u>come</u> when I'm out there! You hear me man? Like splish-splash! An' you, you got no idea- none! How hot it gets. Just the energy alone could kill ya! There's ten, twenty thousand of 'em chargin' at you in a sea of hunger. An' when they hit! WOW! Watch out! 'Cause they want! Need! Little feel, a touch! Yeah, cops try an' keep 'em back, sure. But they keep pushin', yellin', "JOHN-NY! JOHN-NY!"

So all I can do, all I got left is to put it out, s'fast as I can. Give 'em what they want. From deep inside. But s'never enough! No! So I sing-scream from my balls, which are bursting! Try to touch 'em any way I can. To connect! Like in some huge, massive intimacy!

An' I'll tell ya man, I'm like outta control out there. S'like I'm in some strange, dark, twilight zone land where there's wild fire screams. Them callin' my name, "JOHN-NY! JOHN-NY!!" Heat an' energy's exploding. Lights bombarding me from every angle, illuminatin' this insanity where the demands are MON-U-MENTAL! Where any second I feel like I'm gonna snap! Pop! An' those sounds I make, s'not music No! They're howls! HOWLS AMPLIFIED! Me to them, cage to cage- sayin', "We're not alone. We're all here together!" S'like some epic pagan ritual a love! Rock and roll! Rock an roll, kids! An' I'm just a singer in a band doin' a gig. Isn't that a goof? Cause that's all it is. That's all I am. I'm no Pied Piper, no. I'm just a singer... singing in a band.

30's-50's - A street corner. After a torrential
summer rain, Jeb, a homeless man meets up
with his friend Zack. The two get drunk
together and Zack tells Jeb about a miracle
that occurred during the storm. Here Jeb
shares Zacks story.

Was one of them summer rains that starts out when the
air is warm, an' it's muggy, y'know.
Then there's lightnin'.
An' the skies open up wit' thunder.
An' it pours,
       an' pours.
Till the streets shine from the wet.
An' all the filth seems to float away.
   Down the sewers,
       outta sight.
An' the city becomes like "reborn".
An' after it stops rainin',
   for a short time,
      everything becomes like new,
        an' good.
   Even the people ya pass seem happier- smilin'.
Well,
   I was walkin' in the rain that night.
      Soakin' wet and walkin'
Mindin' my own,
   but observin' as I do
     the people on the Avenue.
When I ran into my ole friend Zack, the blind man.
He was sittin' on a stoop
   drinkin' tequila sunrises outta a brown paper bag.
"Doin' fine, yeah!", he said.
  Celebratin'. Full a life!
     Laughin' by himself.
      Singin' up a sermon!
   Talkin' 'bout how "The Assembly a Saints" come down
        durin' the storm.
   They'd come,

he said,
>to help folks "crossover".

"Yeah", Zack said,
>"them in pain or with problems are gonna forget 'em
for tonight 'cause the Assembly a Saints are linin' up on the
Avenue.
>Gonna reach out to folks.
>Gonna give 'em a hand!
>Gonna help folks to "crossover!"

Then he starts to laugh.
>An' no one can laugh like Zack.
>An' like a bubble bouncin' between us,
>>I joined in.

An' we laughed,
>An' laughed good!

Just laughed an' laughed an' laughed!
>"Happy days is comin'.", Zack said
>"Don'cha see it Zeb?! Reach out ya arms an' feel!"

An' I did.
>I reached out.
>>An' Zack was right!

Somethin' had happened in the rain.

Was jus' like Zack said.
>An' we laughed ourselves into the night,
>>me an' Zack.

>Laughed an' laughed!
>>The two of us,
>>>drinkin' tequila sunrises out of a brown
>>>>paper bag.

Two of us,
>crazy drunk,
>sittin' there.

Jus' feelin' the rain,
>an' singin'
to the Assembly a Saints,
>on the Avenue.

20's- a trench in Vietnam during the war. It's Christmas in Vietnam. Juan and a buddy are in the trenches, stoned. Here Juan tells his friend about a Christmas at home.

You gotta come there some day man. Fuckin' Christmas s'crazy. Everyone's there. People all over. Wall to wall. Neighbors, family, kids. Cake, candy, food everywhere. Poppy be always wearin' the same suit- twenty years. An' momma, wait'll you meet her, man. Mama's a trip. She's beautiful. Big girl, momma. Must be I bet, two hundred, two hundred fifty pounds. And at Christmas she always wears her red beaded dress. Cut real low. Very sexy.

An' so we all get drunk. All of us. Whole family. Even the kids, yeah. Pina Coladas, Egg Nog, whatever. Shitfaced! Twisted! Do some reefer, get stoned. T.V.'s on, music's blasting. Perry Como, Spanish Christmas carols, Ave Maria, whatever. Toys all over the place. Gifts opened, wrapping paper, shit like that. Everyone yellin', singin', dancin'. Man, you should see. An' there's mama in her hot red dress, wobblin' aroun', tryin' to keep it together. Set the table. Takes her forever.

Well finally, s'time to eat. An' we're all starvin'. Everyone charges the table, scramblin' for seats. An' Carmen comes in carryin' the turkey. Everybody oohs an' aahs. But Carmen's as shitfaced as everyone else. An' the turkey starts slippin' an' slidin' off a the tray till it fuckin' falls all over everything. INSTANT FIASCO! Kids go crazy! Start grabbin' for it. Playin' with it, the turkey, like it's a fuckin' football. Keeps slidin' outta their hands. Grease, gravy all over the place. Then momma starts gettin' hysterical. Poppy laughs so hard he pees in his pants. Momma finally jus' gives up. An' we all get fuckin' hysterical. Twisted! We all go fuckin' crazy! S'a scene an' a half. I'm tellin' ya. Fuckin' Christmas, man, you gotta see. Shit, yeah... yeah.

20's-40's - a singles bar. Marty Cool thinks of himself as Mr. "It", the make out man. He hasn't quite realized yet what a jerk he is, and how his come on is really a big turn off.

(trying to be the ultra smooth talker)
When I saw you
    over here,
        I knew.
            I knew, like ying-yang,
                That's her.
                    She's <u>it!</u>
My "fair lady" awaits.
S'like chemical attractions happen.
    All the time.
    Every day.
    Aren't we proof?
        In life,
            there's just some women who "sing your song".
            And you,
                you do mine.
Why even way across the bar,
   in this quiet little corner,
      where you were shyly hiding
        I noticed you.
   An' then,
        I knew.
            We played a little "peek-a-boo".
               I saw you—
                  then you-
                  saw me.
Our eyes—
    through the smoke.
      We smiled,
        made contact,
           like in some movie.
An' timing's everything.
            Everything!
               So I made the quick dash over.

Doin' a beeline through the drunks
in this over-raucous crowd.
Full speed ahead!
Like Moses through the parting sea.
Just to be
next to you.
All because-
I knew.
Something inside me
kept saying,
"GO!
GO!
It's meant to be."
And was after our "How'd cha do's".
small talk,
was then,
I knew- Yes!
She's special.
Not just another
Miss somebody else,
sitting alone,
having a drink.
Some lonely lady,
on a Saturday night-
Not you!
You're "magic".
Whatt'sa matter?
Where ya goin'?
What I say?
I'll hold your seat, okay?
Miss!
Miss?!
Where. . .?
(to himself) What I say?!
Where'd she go?!
WHAT I DO?!
What?
WHAT?!

20's-40's a small room at the State of Grace Motel. Planning on going on a shooting spree, Jeremy, an unhappy, somewhat mentally disturbed man, starts drinking and planning his strategy

(Jeremy stares straight out. His eyes are glazed, a cigarette drips from his lips. On the table is a half empty bottle of bourbon, a nearly empty glass, an ashtry filled with smoked cigarette butts, and some empty packs of cigarettes. He speaks slowly.)

Stayin' at the State A Grace Motel. Bible in the drawer, color T.V., little fridge on the floor. Not much but ya can't beat the price, I'll tell ya. An' what's best, that which I most appreciate is that they leave you a-lone. A-lone! Luxury in itself now a days. Come here to hang out with my deepest thoughts. Gonna take some magic rides inside (he smiles).

I'm here, middle a nowhere, miles from the main road, for one thing and one thing only- to come to terms. Deal with the Edgar Allen Poe kina thoughts I've been thinkin' lately. The spooky ones. Thoughts that got me locked up with devils in the cellar. But tonight's gonna be a summit! Gonna stir 'em up till they come upstairs. Here, where it's nice an' solitary. Gonna enter the war. Battle lines set. Gonna meet the enemy head on. Gonna take a gun, (he demonstrates, using his fingers) hold it up to his head, an' whoever he is, stare him in the eyes-real close. An' then BOOM! BOOM! An' it's durin' the boom that the nows gonna hit the then. It's then that all them liars in sheeps clothing that made a path through my life, that mud puddle a people, gonna be EMULSIFIED!

Talkin' about an expose! Just like in True Confidential. Right here, in this room, 'fore your very eyes. Here at the State a Grace Motel, where ya can't beat the price, but there ain't no view

Tonight we play cards, divy up and sort out the who's who.

An' jus so you know- to underline it, make it perfectly clear. I'm here at the State a Grace... I've come... to come to terms.

50's-60's at the kitchen table. For a year, since their son died of Aids, Vernice has hardly said a word to Dave. He's tried everything to break down her wall but was only left frustrated. Here he finally releases his pent up feelings by telling his wife now he felt their son really died.

S'amazing he ever knew anything, your son! You were always on top of him- like a blanket! Always over protecting. Who could get near him?! Boy couldn't breathe. Couldn't breathe! Twenty-eight years old an' still leavin' home. That's normal by you?! Livin' with ya mother an' father, twenty-eight years old?!

You wanna know how he died?! How he really died?! I been sittin' here for a year waitin' for you. Waitin' for you to talk- say somethin'. Anything! But no- nothin'! Turned your back on me. So now it's my turn, an' I'll tell ya. I'll tell ya how our son died. 'Cause he didn't just die of the Aids. No! Started way before that. Took a whole lifetime, Vernice. You worked on that kid every day since he was born. Every single day! Always making sure. Never letting go! Till he couldn't breathe. Was suffocating. Had to run away. Had too! Have a secret life, hide himself, run to the city. You wanna know how he died?! I'll tell you. You! You did it! You smothered him, Vernice. Smothered him to death!

30's-50's Anywhere. Mark has a very unusual encounter with a beautiful woman in the elevator of his office building. Here he recalls that encounter in erotic detail.

(He wears a conservative suit. Warm and friendly)
She walked into the elevator very slowly. Looked. Smiled. Nice, Very nice. I smiled back. Polite and friendly. She was a real cutie. Little blonde. Conservatively dressed. Three piece suit. 'Bout five three, five four. Carrying a black shoulder bag, New York Times. You get the picture. Class act. I figure she's one of the exec. secretaries here. It's a big building. Haven't seen everyone. Maybe she's new.

Anyway, she walks in, pushes her button, leans on the rear wall, next to me. Right next to me. Almost touches me, that close. We check each other out. She flashes me another gorgeous smile. I'm in love- instantly! Ready for the ride. Let's play. I smile back, little more friendly. Little less polite. Door to the elevator closes. Slam! We're on our way. And just when I'm about to make some small talk. Say, "Hi", something like that, I notice she's staring directly at my crotch. Really! Intensely staring. I kid you not. I'm carrying a container of coffee, figured I spilled some. Look down, nothing. Look up, she's still staring. Big smile on her face. Staring right at it! Somethin's going on. Elevator stops. She leans back. Looks up at the floor display. So do I. Like nothing happened. Door opens. Messenger boy walks in. Black guy, early twenties, spandex pants, little hat, wearing a walkman, sunglasses, and a big smile. We all do little hello's. He presses his floor, turns around, door closes again. We're on our way. But this time, when the elevator starts, the blonde quickly moves right in front of me. Yeah! Starts backing up. Like a car into a parking space. Right into me. I'm shocked! Can't believe what's happening. Backs right up until she's snug. Very snug. Compressed. I can feel her panties through my suit. I can smell her perfume. Feel her breathing in and out against me. Messenger boy's oblivious to the whole thing. Got his walkman turned up high. I'm starting to sweat. It's getting hot. Then hands. Hands! She puts her hands behind her back. First one, then the other. They start feeling their way. Oh my God! Up my legs, thighs, until she finds my zipper. Working fast. Then she opens it. My zipper! I don't believe it! Elevator's hurling us up. Express. Fifteenth floor, then twenty. Her fingers find what they're looking for. And she starts playing with me. Playing it like a flute. Bloods rushing. I don't believe this! My coffee's spilling all over the place. She turns around. Has this incredible smile on her face. An awkward moment. What do you say?! What do you say to a woman who's fondling you? Giving you a hand job in an elevator?! Then she goes from playing the flute to playing the tuba. Boom-ba-boom! Intense! Then she yells out, "This how you like it?!" Immediately the messenger boy turns around, catches us! Oh my God! He quickly presses the emergency button. Alarm goes off. Everything stops, including her. Oh no! She moves away. And the three of us just stare at each other as the alarm loudly rings.

I cover myself, zip up, embarrassed. Tell the messenger boy, "Hey man, she's my girlfriend. S'how she likes to get off." He smiles. I fumpher, keep fumphering. Making a fool of myself.

And he just keeps going, "Uh-huh. Uh-huh."

Someone yells from upstairs, "You okay down there?"

Messenger boy yells back, "We fine man, but the elevators stuck."

"Just stay calm", they say. "Be about fifteen minutes. Just hold on."

Messenger boy looks at me, smiles. Then real softly, "So... how ya like her, huh? She's good, right?"

What?!

"An you just had the comin' attractions. S'a whole show waitin'. For fifty, ya get the whole thing."

What?! WOW! OH MY GOD!

The messenger boy puts his finger on the emergency button. "So, whatiya say, Mister? Wanna come? Or do we go?"

I take a sip of what's left of my coffee, look at her, she smiles.

"Fifty?" I say.

"Fifty. Got about fifteen minutes worth."

I smile. "Guess I just tell the boss I got stuck in the elevator. Shit happens." I take out my wallet, hand him the money. He takes it, turns around, turns on his walkman.

I lean on the rail, finish my coffee. As the blonde, the cute little blonde... takes it home.

Any age - anywhere. Paulie, a two-bit loser, tries to convince an old friend to invest in a show.

(High charged)
This show...
   This show... I'm tellin' ya...
         s'gonna be great!
            Unbelievable!
               Spectacular! - You'll see!
  S'gonna have great sets!
      Costumes galore!
         Electric gizmos everywhere!
Wait!
  Gonna have actors,
       singers,
           hot lookin' dancers- wearin' practically
nothin! And high wire acts- naked! NAKED!
Doin' unbelievable things up there.
Unbelievable!
Things you never seen before!
All lit up
by lazer lighting- with jels on 'em.
That'll enhance these moments of super-high-charged drama
      that will occur
         on this GARGANTUOUS STAGE.
      Astounding every one
        of the over-vast audience
        of high priced ticket buyers below.
Who will have
      FOUGHT FOR,
           KILLED FOR
             tickets to our show.
Our event!
  EXTRAVAGANZA!
That nobody thought could happen.
(almost a whisper) But it will.
We're gonna make it happen.
Us.
  WE

are gonna take them
on a pre-planned magical journey
the likes of which no one has ever seen before.
Listen to me- I know. I KNOW!
An' I'm no shmo- you know that.
No pipe dream
dreamer.
My feet are on the ground. BOTH OF 'EM!
Just LOOK!
IMAGINE!
SEE IT!
Then give me your hand,
a couple a G's,
an we're set.
Open your eyes!
I'm talkin' HIGH POTENTIAL!
MEGA-POSSIBILTY!
Future greatness for both of us!
And I'm letting you in
ground floor.
Don't cling to your piggy bank- not now!
This is the big one. The BIG BANANA!
Take us both to the top- and beyond.
Trust me.
Trust me on this like you never have.
If for no other reason. . .
(sincerely) because I'm your best friend.
And I love you kid. You know that.
I'd never let you get hurt. Never!
You can count on me
Ya know...
you're like a brother to me.
You are.
A big brother.
And brothers
never let each other down- right?
And this show
is for the both of us.
For our friendship.

I love ya kid.
        You know that.
whatiya say?

30's-50's - a mid town bar. Sam thought he'd seen it all. It's very difficult to shake up a mid town bartender. But one night a mysterious stranger came into his bar and everything changed.

He came in through that door — there. Yeah. Just like anybody else. But I knew him. Hmm. Immediately.

Place was quiet. Piano man was playing some bluesy number I think. An' I was settin' up as usual. Gettin' ready for the late night crowd. An' in he came. Sat right here, next to me at the bar. Those strange dark eyes, an' that smile. That smile! I smiled back — nice, easy, no problem.

He ordered a scotch. I served him. Why the hell not? I'm the bartender, right? S'my job. S'what I do. But I knew, yeah, it was gonna be an interestin' night. Hot times folks. Fun. Fun! He'd come to town, and was perched on that bar stool like a spider. Havin' a smoke, blowin' smoke rings, slowly sippin' his drink. Cruisin' for a playmate. All smiles... an' waitin'. His eyes, intense and deep.

Who's he gonna get?

How's he gonna charm 'em?

What'll be his line tonight?

An' I was like some schoolboy fascinated by the master. An' he loved bein' the show. Yeah. I was drawn to his energy. His... sexual power. Red. Hot! Self-contained. His movements slow, sensuous, attracting. Pulling me in. An' I was... losing control.

The bar was steaming with this hot, blue mist. An' all of us, all of us here, like fell under his influence— the Master of the Night.

Then he turned to me — opened his arms, and gave a big belly laugh. He grabbed me, pulled me right out from behind the bar, gave me a big hug, an' whispered, (softly) "Dance with me son. Listen to the music." I was chosen and... I gave in.

An' as we slowly danced, he whispered, (softly) "Heaven and hell are the same place. The only difference is the door you enter." Then he kissed me on the lips—here. The music stopped — like that! An' he let go. Was off dancin' with someone else from the bar; as the music began again. An' I stood there watchin' him dance, rubbing my lip. As he slowly went from one to another — touching us all. All of us. Igniting... something.

Eventually, we'd all have our stories to tell about that night... and many others. Yeah. Those moments in the bars, in the beds, on the streets. Those times we could all say we knew, an' danced with, an' kissed... the Devil.

30's-50's - anywhere. Bill, a story line writer for a soap opera tells of how he finally learned to deal with the pressure of a deadline.

My producer was on my back. The sponsor was on hers. It was uh-oh time! Constant phone calls back and forth.

"Got anything?! Got anything?!"

"Not yet! Need more time!", I tried to calm her, get her to relax, but she'd just hang up.

Was only early afternoon but seemed like everyone was running for cover. The ratings had dropped again. We'd just lost Boston and Idaho, two big markets. Everyone knew the show was on the skids. Heads were about to roll.

When it hits the fan like that, only way I can break through the barbed wire- is go south. Disappear, find a bar, have a few- and pray.

So within an hour I was three scotches to the wind in some dump on the upper east side bending some bartenders ear. Telling him of the injustices, the tortures of the damned that a deadline could put you through.

The bartender, a good listener, gave a knowing smile. Said he knew all about it. Wrote down the name and address of a bar. Said, "Go there. Tell 'em Al sent you. Al! Just go pal, pronto!" I smiled, paid him, and left. Realized how desperation makes children of us all. How now I was simply following orders. Last hopes. The cab ride, a wing and a prayer to God knows where. Some dead end street in the lower bowels of Manhattan. Somewhere below China town I think. I found the door, knocked. It opened, a large man said, "What?"

I said, "Al sent me. Al!"

He smiled, ushered me in. And inside... inside this dimly lit bar... My God, what a sight! Hundreds of people; all of them in various states of panic. Some running, some screaming and some getting drunk. Was Dantes Inferno, the Snake Pit and New York Stock Exchange all rolled into one.

A small man with large eyes, dark circles under them, approached me.

"What times yours?!, he said.

41

"My what?"

"Deadline! DEADLINE!"

"Oh... uh, six o'clock", I said.

He scowled, said "Six?! You got plenty of time!" He pointed to the walls. They were covered with clocks. Hundreds and hundreds of them. All kinds- some ticking, some not.

"I'm down to the last minutes", he said. "Last few. Then it's the end of the line!" Then he ran off screaming, poor guy.

Some college kids came running by, yelling something about term papers due tomorrow, but not even started yet.

A woman in a fur coat, who was about to have a cocktail party; guests arriving soon. But she hadn't ordered any food or liquor yet. She was getting drunk- beginning to panic.

A bride, getting married in the morning, still hadn't bought her gown yet. Couldn't decide.

All of them- terrified. The Deadline bar was filled with adrenalin and anxiety. And I seemed to fit right in.

Was then I noticed on the floor a large white line that absolutely no one stepped on. And like Alice's rabbit I started to follow; see where it led. It meandered through the crowd. Led up to a door near the back of the bar. Slowly I pushed it open. Inside was the scowling man I'd just met, standing in front of this huge clock. He was holding a gun to his head. He turned to me. In his eyes a look- a plea. I understood. Desperation. But what could I. . .? There was nothing... I was as helpless as him!

Seeing this, he turned back to the immense clock like a disciple before a shrine. Then this incredibly loud alarm went off. DEAFENING! I held my hands to my ears. He cocked the gun, pulled the trigger, and screamed! (pause) A little red flag popped out of the gun, said, "Bang! Bang! You're dead."

Then he fell down on the floor. Just laid there motionless.

Then... he started to laugh. Really laugh! Loudly! Like he'd heard the funniest joke ever! And I noticed that he'd landed on the line. The white line on the floor.

The... deadline! Of course! It was the deadline. HE'D PASSED THE DEADLINE... AND NOTHING HAPPENED! Bang-bang, you're dead. I realized why he was laughing. And I started to laugh too. All of a sudden it seemed very funny. The whole thing. All of it. The soap, my producer, everything! You pass a deadline and nothing! Life goes on. Let 'em shoot me! So what?!

I stood there a few minutes more- laughing with him. Then closed the door and left. Went back home- walked, all the way. When I got there I sat at my desk, turned on the typewriter, and typed up a storm.

20's- 30's - the Rosenstein kitchen in Brooklyn. Here Michael tells his brother how he learned and accepted that he had Aids.

I kept hoping, y'know? Kept... For months. But I knew. I just... losing weight, tired all the time. Mom kept saying, "Mickey, you're getting so thin. What's wrong?" Telling her, "It's just stress. Don't worry ma." Telling myself it's this or that. Any excuse, one after another. But then I ran out of things. No reasons left. So finally I went to the doctor, took the test.

Then last night, sitting there in his waiting room- forever. Making all kinds of deals with myself. Promises, y'know. If only... Anything... I'll be good. But when he came in, was walking towards me... the look in his eyes Barry, I'll never forget. Game was over. The doctor didn't have to say a thing... I knew.

30's-40's - anywhere. Last night Claire met a handsome stranger at the fruit and vegetable stand. Here she excitedly recalls their meeting.

Meetin' Hank, oh my, was like meetin' Mr. Perfect- Mr. Love at First Sight. End of the rainbow. Late last night at the fruit and vegetable stand down the street. Mr. Kees. Mr. Kees on the corner. Mr. Kees got the best produce around. Everyone knows. Anyway, there was Hank holding a comice pear in his hand. An' I was standin' right next to him checkin' out the summer peaches. Peaches an' pears, funny huh? Like it was pre-ordained. An' Hank said, "Scuse me Ma'am. You know anything about these?" I looked up an' almost dropped my peaches, I swear. He was so good lookin'. A ten. A real ten! Tall, dark, tan-that kina thing. Great bod, wearin' bermuda shorts. An' eyes... eyes that kina looked right through ya. I smiled kina coy. Said, "Well, whatiya needa know?"

"How can ya tell...? How ya know if they're fresh?", he asked.

"Gotta squeeze. Squeeze 'em", I said. "Shouldn't be hard. Soft is sweet."

He smiled. I just melted. Was like in the movies. Robert Redford meets Doris Day at a fruit stand. I... touched his pear, said, "Now don't squeeze too hard. Ya gotta be gentle. It's delicate."

"I can see", he said, lookin' right inta my eyes. I almost keeled over.

"Definitely delicate", he said. "I wouldn't hurt it for anything." I felt a warm breeze pass right through me like I wasn't even there.

"What's ya name?", he asked.

I put my peaches down, looked up, and said, "Claire. My name's Claire."

"Hi there Claire, I'm Hank."

"Hi Hank".

I could see Mr. Kee smiling from behind the cash register. Seemed like all the fruits were glowin'- brightly!

"I just moved to New York", Hank said. "Don't know

anybody yet. An' this town's a big place. Ya know what I mean? It's very, very big."

"Oh yes Hank I know exactly what'cha mean. I do. I definitely do. This place swallows a up if ya don't watch out. Can make ya feel invisible sometimes. Like people are walkin' right through ya. Like ya don't even exist. Believe me, I know."

"Yeah", he said. "That's the feelin'".

I felt my fingers tremble. Not knowin' what to do next. An' my breath, I know my breath just stopped mid air between us. We both stood there under Mr. Kees bright lights holdin' our fresh fruit with frozen smiles. One horribly long pause. Cash register rang. A bus went by. The bubble finally broke when Hank said, "Guess I'll see ya Claire. Thanks for ya help."

"Was nothin' Hank. Anytime."

As he walked away I slowly began to wither and die. Just die. I crushed a peach in my fingers. Thought, "No, not again. Not again! How long have I...? Damn it! I have taken too many late night walks down to Mr. Kees to let someone like Hank just walk away. This out-of-town, just arrived, "miracle".

I called out, "Hank. Hey Hank!"

He turned around.

"Why don'cha give me a call? I'll take ya on an insiders tour of the Big Apple."

He smiled a big smile. Ear to ear. Said, "I'd like that Claire. I really would."

"Well then just give me a call", I said. I gave him my number, he paid for his fruit, and left.

Mr. Kee smiled from behind the cash register.

"Tonight good?", he said.

"Oh yes, Mr. Kee", I smiled back. "Tonight, very good. Tonight was the best!"

Any Age - Anywhere. Patrice was an abused child. Here she describes her special fantasy place. The place she went when in danger.

(Gently, dreamy)
My hands
    gently drip
    off the side
        of a soft green avocado cloud-
            floating in the middle of a blue, blue sky.
Miles and miles above anything.
    Slowly,
        I let my long rubbery arms
                drift
                    all the way down
                        to the earth
                            far below.
        Where I soak my long, elastic fingers.
            Let them cool off.
                One by one
                    in the crisp cool
                        of a Vermont waterfall.
Nothing hurts.
    Nothing at all.
        Paradise!
(with growing apprehension)
                            But...
somewhere in the distance
                        is a sound.
Somewhere
    on the edge,
        near a canyon,
                a sound- like thunder.
    Or perhaps
        it's a herd of wild animals.
    I don't know.
Or maybe...
            maybe the earth is cracking. It's that loud.
So very loud it scares me.

'Cause it's coming closer.
                    MY GOD!
(Becoming terrified)
I know I have to move- soon!
Run! Yes!
Jump away!
          Off the cloud!
                    Come back.
I know I have to open my eyes soon.
                    Feel again.
                    Come back.
                         Here
                              to my room.
                                   Here,
                                        with him,
                                             Daddy.

Here, where everything is so loud.
His voice-
          yelling!
                    Bouncing off the walls.
                         As he hits me
                              again
                                   and again.
                                        The strap- it hurts!
                                        My fingers are swollen.
                              DON'T DADDY-DON'T ! !

But the sound
     the belt and buckle.
               And the look of rage
                    as the light hits his eyes.
As he keeps hitting me.
               Hitting!
My hands
   try to cover my face.
                    To protect.
               No daddy- DON'T!
               No more!
                    Please!
                         No more!

49

I'll be good!
(Changing back to dreamy)
Until finally...
      a cloud
         floats by.
            And I leap to my rescue.
            My own rescue.
            Drift away- leave.
Till I'm miles and miles above the room
              looking down.
Till I can't see or feel
         anything.
Just
  the lovely
      blue
        blue
          sky.
             Quiet.
Where I feel my fingers
        soothed in the cool water.
As I wait,
    and drift.
        Just drift.
          Drift away.
           Until
             I hear the door slam.
              And he leaves-
                has left.
And my cloud slowly floats back to my room.
        To my bed-
          soft,
           safe.
    Safe.
        Where I can close my eyes.
         And finally
            fall
              asleep.

40's-60's - An executive office. Margerie is a successful, always direct, in control, executive. She has just been given an ultimatum by the board of directors of her company. Here, she shares her feelings with a secretary.

No where fast. S'like walking up a down escalator. Till you start running. But then the escalator picks up speed. Steps go by faster. Till you feel like you're not moving; that there's no point. But you don't give up. You can't! Just keep pushing! Somehow knowing— refusing to give up. Yet as fast as you run- the escalator keeps picking up speed. Steps fly by faster and faster. Till you're running for your life. But it feels like you're going backwards. No movement- none! Sweat dripping off of you. Knowing if you break, falter, stop for one second—I mean a half a moment, it will overtake you. And not only will you lose, but you'll be pulled in, sucked up like a piece of dirt- crushed between the metal steps. So all I have is my will, don't you see? My determination! The God damn need to... And as far as...

Every morning, when I wake up... a knot... in my stomach. Before I take my first breath... My gut feeling... Don't you think I know?! You think I'm stupid?! I'm a woman, like you, and they resent us! They do! They don't like it! How dare I?! Well, I'm sorry. I'm sorry, but... But!!

Now they can accept the status quo, with me, where I am-as is... AS IS!! Or they can all, each one of them, jump out a god-damn window! Because I'm not going anywhere! I worked to hard to get here. S'taken to long. And my time is worth much more. Much more! So no damn board of directors or anyone- Anyone! - is going to tell me which way the escalator goes!

So you can just go back in there, tell your bosses if they want me, want to talk, tell them I'm here. Right here! In my office, behind my desk. And if they want me, they know where to look!

30's-40's Anywhere. Each night, when everyone in her family is asleep, Tonya takes her nightly bubble bath. It is there that she allows her "wings" to come out. Here she talks about the journeys she takes, her night flights.

(sweetly, gently)

I have these tiny tuck-a-way wings that I only take out at night. At night, when everyone's asleep. When the house is quiet. When I take my bubble bath. Soapy suds. It's then that I allow them out. My wings. By lifting my arms and breathing. Taking deep breaths, spreading... spreading until one by one, out they plop- my wings. Soft, white, majestic. I stand up, stare at myself in the mirror. Naked, with only the light of a candle. I look like a goddess- an angel in a painting. So regal! And I spread my wings, the soap suds dripping off them. Spread them wider and wider until they almost touch the walls. Then I slowly get out of the tub, dry off and powder. One last look in the mirror, then I slowly open the bathroom door. Peak out, listen. Quiet. Blow out the candle, then tip toe through the living room, carefully checking every step of the way. Making sure no one's up. Tip toe to the window. Slowly open it. Feel the warm night on my naked skin. How cool it feels. Open the window to the top, look up at the moon, and smile. Start getting excited. Soon. One last look back. Then I leap to the ledge, and gently, quietly push off into the night. The feel of it! The freedom! That first leap! I spread my wings and glide. Press against the wind. Glide! Then push down and fly. Fly! Higher and higher. Into the night. Can anything be better than this? Higher! Above the buildings. My wings push down against the air. The coolness. Then faster, faster! Up. Out. Careful of antennas, rooftops. Higher, higher, into the clouds. Kicking, spreading my arms. Feeling the mist. The coolness of the night. My shadow on a cloud. The moon up above. For hours and hours, total freedom, Playing. Fun. Until... that moment. In the distance, that first pin point of light. The first sign that it's the end of the night. And I must return. Slowly, sadly, back own. Like falling- going home.

Back. Lowering myself. Down. Down. Returning home. Home. Until I'm back. Right outside the window, peaking in. Making sure everything's still quiet inside. Then back onto the ledge. Look in. Then tip toe back through the living room. Making sure everyone's still asleep. Yes. Then back into the tub. Some soap suds still left. Water's still warm. As I begin to wash off the night. But still savor the memories. Soak. Soak. Relax, and slowly get ready for the new day.

Any age - sitting at a table. Laura has found something that's changed her life. Here she talks to another woman about it. As she talks she constantly smiles and seems genuinely happy.

For me, it was like the end of a long night. Coming out of a tunnel or something. Seeing people waiting there, welcoming you. People who understood- cared. People who'd been there.

I mean before, my life... my life was okay. It was. Just seemed to go by, day after day. I'd go to work, go out, date, see friends, vacation. It was fine- really. Didn't seem to bad. But just... never seemed right on the money if you know what I mean. There was something... unsatisfying. Not complete. Like a record that kept skipping. I couldn't hear the whole melody.

(then) Would you like some more tea? You sure? I can just... Okay.

(Back to story) So, then, one night Christina called. Seemed very excited about something. Said she couldn't talk on the phone. Could I come over. Sure. So I did. And when I got there she introduced me. I met Elja. Isn't she lovely? Yeah. And from the very first moment, there was just something- so warm. At first, I had trouble understanding her- her accent. Then, as she went on, told me about it, I'll tell you, my first impulse was to run away. I thought, no, this is dangerous. This is terrifying! I should leave. I wanted to... but then I noticed Christina standing there. Noticed how she'd changed. She was like a whole different person. Then I met Susan, Mary Beth, all the others. And there was such love in the room. Genuine, real, warmth. A caring. They all seemed... so happy. So genuinely happy. Christina, who's usually not very... well, she'd changed. I'd never seen her... so glowing. And they all sat with me, helped me to realize. Encouraged me. Told me about the "new world". Happiness. Just within my reach. And it was all so simple. So very simple. And forever. The rest of my life. For as long as I lived. And with no side effects. None. (She takes out a small bottle, opens it, takes out a small white pill, holds it) What amazes me the most is how quickly it works. Just one pill, and in a few minutes you fall asleep. And when you wake up... you're in a garden. A lovely, constantly blooming, beautiful garden. It really is exactly what they call it, "the miracle pill from Brazil". I don't know how it works. Doesn't really matter. All I know is the last few weeks my life... I smile... Every thought I have... It's wonderful! Now I hear music all the time. A lovely, on-going, melody. Sweet, tender moments. I still do what I did before. Same job, everything. But, I don't know, I just... laugh, a lot. Always seem to be having a great time. And I smile... at myself, inside. (She smiles, then softly) What have you got to lose? (She puts the pill on the table) Look at it. See, it's just a little pill. What's to be afraid of? It can only do you good, believe me. What do you say? (a pause) Good. (she smiles) I'm so happy for you. Now when you take it, take a good gulp of tea. A good gulp. S'like Elja always says, "Sometimes... sometimes happiness is the hardest pill to swallow."

30's-60's - Rosas kitchen. Here Rosa, a hearty
Italian housewife, tells an amazing story about
a wooden madonna that cried blood tears, and
the effect it had on her family.

I never seen nothin' like it. Listen, wait. We're eatin',
me an' Tony. Just finished the tortellini, when Gino, Maria's
kid comes runnin' in. Says he found somethin' he gotta show
us. I said, "In a minute, Gino. How's ya momma? Want
somethin' to eat?"

But he's like in a panic, Gino. The look in his eyes! "Ya
gotta see this!", he says. "Ya gotta see!"

"What, Gino?! What's so special?" Tony gets upset;
excited. I could see his blood pressure risin'. "Can'chu see
we're eatin', huh?! Don'chu see?!", he says.

I calmed Tony down, says, "What is it Gino? What do
you gotta show us?"

An' Gino holds up this box. Little wooden box. Says
there's a madonna inside.

"Wha'?!"

"A madonna cryin' blood", he says.

"Gino, what are you talkin?! Ya shouldn't talk like that!
S'a sin!"

"But it's true!", he says. Found it down at the empty lot.
"All these birds was flyin' over it. Hundreds a big, black
birds." He thought maybe it was a hit. That maybe there
was a dead body. But was jus' this box lyin there, with the
madonna.

Tony stops eatin' the tortellini. Grabs the box outta
Ginos hand. "Let's see!", he says. Pushes the dishes over, an'
opens the box. An' we all look- Tony, Gino an' me. An'
inside... inside, just like Gino said, is a small, hand carved,
madonna. Musta been the size a my fist. Lovely, petite,
made outta like a white wood. Fragile, delicate. An' like
Gino says, drippin' from her eyes, little, red tears- like blood.
Very slow, one after another. I can't tell ya. Them tears,
that moment.

My heart just broke. I never... I looked over at Tony.
Even Tony... all this emotion goin' on inside a him. Thought

he was gonna cry right then an' there. An very softly, Tony says, "Gino, go get Father Bob. Hurry!" An' Gino left.

We sat there at the table, me an' Tony. Just sat, an watched the madonna cry. Was like a shrine!

I said, "Tony, whatiya think it means?"

Tony didn't answer me. Didn't say a word. An' I never saw where Tony didn't have somethin' to say. An' the look on his face, you shoulda seen. Such emotion goin' on inside him. Was like when little Antony was born. The day Tony first saw him in the hospital. Such... deep feelins'.

Then all of a sudden, he got beet red. Grabbed for his chest, like he couldn't breathe. Then he fell over, right off the chair.

I screamed, "Tony!", grabbed for him, but was too late. He hit his head on the table, an' fell, layin' there on the linoleum. Sprawled out on the kitchen floor- not moving. Nothin'. I went over, touched him. An' I knew, just knew... he was dead. Couldn't believe it. Just a couple a minutes before, we're sittin there, havin tortellini, an' now..

Father Bob comes rushin' in, looks down, sees Tony lyin' there. An' I was like hysterical, outta my mind, tryin' to tell him what happened. Was amazin' I could even talk. Then father Bob starts with the last rites. As I'm screamin' my good-bye's to Tony. Tellin' him what a good husband he was. What a good father. Everything!

In the middle of the commotion Gino went over to the table. He got the box with the madonna, brought it over to us, sat down with Father Bob an' me, an' opened it. When he did I just... I don't know. I looked over for some reason. Then I stopped cryin'. Just stopped, like for no reason. An' Father Bob, he stopped givin' the rites. Room was so quiet you could hear a pin drop. All of us sat there, looking down at the madonna.

An' then... get ready, Tony sat up! You heard me, just sat up. Started rubbin' his head, askin' what happened.

Me, Gino, and Father Rob looked at him like he was Christ come back from the dead; our mouths dropped! Then I started huggin' him, kissin him, tellin' him how much I love him. Father Bob started pattin' him on the back. An' little

Gino just sat there laughin. Found it funny, I guess.

An' then we all of us, like at the same time, looked down at the madonna in the box. An' ya know what? The madonna had stopped cryin'!

**20's-50's - a hospital cafeteria, about two a.m.
Shelly, a nurse, rambles as she tries to express
her feelings about the loss of a young patient.**

Care? Caring? Too much, I don't know. Is that
possible? Don't we...? I mean, we're all concerned. Supposed
to be, right? But there should be a distance, I know.
Professional. Always. A professional distance. I know. I
know. But some of them get through the lines, the cracks.
You must have... It's late, I'm sorry, I'm rambling. Just tell
me to shut up. (then) You want some more coffee? (She
starts to get up) No? (She sits back down, looks down at her
cup) Coffee? Who am I kidding? This stuff stinks.
Adrenalin- jump start. But serves a purpose. Like us, huh?
(nervously looking around) You'd think they'd clean this
place up once in a while. I mean it's a god damn hospital!
You'd think... Jesus, listen to me. I sound like a shrew. It's
just... (trying to find the words) It's just... Shit! Rules, you
bend them. I've always... What the hell are...? He needed
me. Do you understand? A kid alone in a hospital. Both his
parents died in the fire. So I came every day. Whenever I
had a break, my day off. We shouldn't, I know. But... His
only other visitor was some old blind woman who only spoke
spanish. And she hardly ever came. So he needed more. He
was just a kid! Burned over seventy percent, d'chu know
that?. Prognosis- slim. But I'll tell you, I'd walk in there...
His eyes lit up. Was like Christmas. The way his eyes... I'd
say, "You're looking a lot better today." And he'd squeeze my
hand... tight. So much life. That's all he needed! Somebody
to say hello, squeeze his hand. Imagine that. Just say
"hello", and it's Christmas. Just say... Tell me to shut up,
will you? I'm not even making sense. Why can't I just let it
go? Why... I just need a good nights... Your too good a
listener, you know that? I better go. See you tomorrow. I'm
in E.R.- early. (She gets up, smiles)

Thanks. Blah-blah-blah. (She is still for a moment.
Looks down at her coffee cup.) Damn! This coffee stinks. It...
It really does. Really.

60's - The kitchen- sitting at the kitchen table Edna's sister Martha is in the hospital dying of a terminal illness. Every day Edna goes to visit her hoping for a miracle. Here Edna tells her husband Murray about her visits.

How is she? Don't ask. The same. Same as always. Same as yesterday, day before. Always the same. She just stares up at the ceilin'. Lies there in that hospital an' talks. Talks to I don't know who. Angels on the ceilin' or somethin'. Who the hell knows who she talks to anymore. Who can understand her? Maybe she's preparin' Murray. Gettin' ready to go. Who knows? She jus' lies there in that bed an' talks. Talks like in baby talk. A conversation to nobody- thin air. An' she don't know nobody anymore. Nobody. She just... I don't know. But I'll tell ya. I'll tell ya Murray. There was a second today... Just a second, where from the corner of her eye, I saw like a glimmer, ya know? She gave me a look, and it was just like old times. An' I remembered that look from way back when. For just one moment Murray, I thought maybe she's gonna snap out of it. Maybe a miracle! Say, "I was jus' pretending Edna. Foolin' around. S'gonna be okay again. Jus' like old times." An' she'd throw the blankets back, jump outta bed, and say, "Come on. Come Edna, let's go shoppin'!" An' we'd grab our bags an' run downtown jus' like we usta. But... was just a look. A look. Meant nothin'. Nothin' at all.

40's-60's - the security office of a an expensive department store. Dora, a very wealthy lady, loves to go "shopping". Having just been arrested for shoplifting, she explains her side of the story to the store detective.

(nervous and upset)

Better than! No-no. I never said... I never said that. Never. She must... I never said that I was better than her. She must have misunderstood. I wouldn't. What I said, what I did say to that young lady was that she should have more respect. More respect, okay? Respect! That was the word I used. I mean I would think it's store policy- customers always right, that kind of thing. I'd imagine you'd train these girls to deal with customers in a more dignified manner. Is that asking too much? Is it?! Let's face it this isn't a five and dime. What you're selling here is style- class. S'why I shop here. Always have. Years and years. So I know when I walk through those doors there, I expect to be treated in a certain manner. I expect that! That's why I shop here. However, I do not _ever_ expect to be accosted by the sales help. As I was by that sales girl; who made accusations. Had the nerve... Accusations! And in the bat of an eye calls store security to arrest me. Create an embarrassing scene. Do you know how humiliated I was out there?! Have you any idea?! Taking me off like that? Like I'm some... Like a common criminal! Some cheap crook! Who does she think she is that girl?! And what kind of store...?! I have been a customer here for more years than ...! This is how I'm repaid?! Public humiliation?! How dare...?!

(Trying to maintain her composure) Look... I have no idea. I really don't. I have no idea how that jewelry got in my bag. I certainly never put it there. If I wanted that gold bracelet, if I did, I'd simply have bought it. Taken out my credit card and paid for it. Same thing with the diamond earrings and the pin. Perhaps, when she... I don't know how they got in there. Some error. Mistake. Maybe they just fell in my bag. That can happen. I mean I have no idea. Perhaps it would be better if you checked up on her- the sales girl.

Maybe... I don't know, maybe she put them in my bag. That's probably how they got there. Wouldn't put it past her. The sales help. Resent. They resent us you know. They do. I'll bet she placed those things in my bag when my back was turned. Check out your help young man. They're the ones. They steal. Everyone knows... You just check her out instead of... I mean do I look like a thief?! Do I?! Well?! Do I?!!

20's-40's - a bar. Henny's just had a run in with
a mugger in her apartment. Here she describes
what happened to a man she's just met.

(Energized, quick chatting)
This city... this city sucks! It sucks, haven't you
noticed?! People move here with high hopes, and what? This
city sucks 'em dry. Believe me, only the strong survive.
Look around. Everywhere you look, what?
(like a litany)
Crackheads and cockroaches.
A Great White Way, that's not, right?
Riff-raff everywhere.
And the potholes- please!
Pimps in doorways- watching, waiting.
Subways filled with men- masturbating!
And for every limo there's lunatic on a rampage.
Murder, drugs, disease- a dime a dozen these days.
So . . .
I come here to this bar- to escape. S'like my sanctuary
My oasis in the middle of the madness. Where I can breathe,
have a drink, take a breath. Meet a friend, talk.
Hi, my name's Henny. Nice to meet you. Yeah, I live
right near here. Down the street, other side. Have a cute
little brownstone. One bedroom, I own. It's nice, cozy.
Can I buy you a drink? No? Not yet? Okay.
So anyway, coming home from work, all I could think
about was a nice hot bath. Maybe some white wine, send out
for Chinese, some T.V. A quiet night- by myself. Maybe read
a book. Call a friend. Chit-chat, girl talk, something like
that. Know what I mean? No big plans. Home. Safe.
Alone.
So I got in, plopped down, pooped out on the couch.
Turned on the T.V. Nothin' on. Never is. D'chever notice?
So I got undressed, turned on the water in the tub, lit some
candles, turned off the lights, got in... and soaked. (a release)
Let myself... go. Off to bubble bath heaven. Water wet
dreams. Miles above this god-damned city. To my
Himalayas in the sky. One eye half opened, watching the

candles flicker. Heaven. Paradise. Divine!

But then... a noise. A sound in the living room. Like someone was there. (a frightened whisper) Oh my God! Did I...? Did I leave the front door opened?! YES! I did! Oh my God!

And just as I stood up, the bathroom door opened. And this man... this big man with big hands and a big head stood there staring.

I asked, (frightened) "What do you want?"

He didn't say a thing, started coming towards me. Now remember, I'm standing there- naked!

He starts grabbing for me with his big hands.

(Softly, desperate) "Please mister, don't.

He started to touch, touch me. And then... then I started to splash. Splash him from the tub. Water, everywhere. Soap suds flying in the air. And I screamed, (big and strong) "Get outta here you son of a bitch!" And then I went wild! Splashing all over the place. Screaming as loud as I could! Splashing! Until the candles went out. And it was pitch black. Just me and him alone in the dark. But I kept screaming. Then I started to punch. My fists swinging in the dark. Waiting to connect. And then I did. I think it was his head, I'm not sure. Heard him cry, "OW!". Then I really let him have it! With all I had! Kept punching, hitting in the dark. Hitting! HITTING! Until the bathroom door opened, and I could hear him running. I grabbed a towel, put on the light, and ran after him. I musta been crazy! When I got to the front door it was wide open. He was gone. I slammed it and stood there- shaking. Oh my God! Oh my God!! I leaned on the door, then collapsed to the floor, just looked up at the ceiling, and said, "WOW!" Then a minute or two later I started to cry. Couldn't stop. Like waves of... He coulda killed me! I... I coulda died. But I fought him. Fought back. Was my own hero!

(After a moment) Crazy, huh? Crazy!

Then I got dressed, walked over here, to my "sanctuary".

Look, I don't usually go over to men I've never met in bars. 'Really But tonight... tonight everythings kina all over the place. Topsy turvy. And you had, have a friendly face and I needed to talk. Thanks for listening. And if you want I'll buy you that drink now. A gift... for being such a good listener. It's funny, but you never know who you'll meet, huh? (a little joke) Even in your own bathroom.

(a beat) God, it's nice to be alive. And it's like I said before, remember? In this city... only the strong survive.

30's-40's - a living room. Terry, a strong, attractive, female cop tells her "friend" about an incident of sexual harassment she recently experienced on the job.

(strong, direct, with guts)

I said, "Look Larry, don't! Okay?! Just don't start! Callin' me a bitch is no solution. Was just my time, that's all. My turn, I'm sorry. But s'fair and square. Up the ladder, down the rope. I punch a clock just like you. Alright, maybe you've done it longer, that's all. But I've worked weekends, late nights, overtime- all of it. All of it, just like you! Blah-blah-blah, blah-blah-blah". But him, Larry, wouldn't listen. Was too agitated, upset. Said he'd had enough. Fuck ERA. No Nancy Drew was gonna tell him what to do. He'd rather start from scratch, he said. Reassignment, walk the beat, whatever.

Nancy Drew, do you believe? Marsha, make me another martini please. Two olives, straight up, thanks hon.

(Continuing) I'll tell ya Marsh, I woulda let him go. Woulda let him go in a minute. Fuck him! But the son of a bitch knows the lay of the land. Knows the office better than anyone. Would take me months Marsh, months. Every file, folder, Larry knows. Every case load, crook, two bit felon, Larry knows who, what, and where. Guy's indispensable. Shit, I don't even know where the Creamora is.

Marsh! I said two olives. Look, you just got one in there. And it's all broken up, squished. C'mon, don't we got another somewhere? Could ya look? Thanks hon. You're a doll.

(Continuing) Okay, so it's Waterloo in the office. Larry wants to leave, but I need him. I say, "Can't we compromise? Come to terms?" Well, Larry gets a big smile on his face. Big ugly smile. Slithers over to me, puts his arms around me. Whispers in a guttery voice that if I gave him some head, a blow job, maybe he'd reconsider. You believe the balls on him?!The nerve?! I leaned back on my desk, gave him a cute little bimbo wink, and carefully turned my tape recorder on. Said, "Sure, let's talk." And boy, did he? Told me where he wanted to do it, when, how'd he'd always wanted to. Real filth. Put a noose around himself like you wouldn't believe. Then I said, "Don't you know it's against regulations?"

"Fuck 'em!", he said. He fooled around with plenty of the girls. Then he let his hand slowly drop till it touched my breast. That was it! BAM! Gave him a quick knee to the crotch. Bulls eye!

"You son of a bitch!", I said. "I'm putting you on report. Sexual harassment of a female superior." I said, "superior" real loud. "SUPERIOR!" Then I pulled out the tape recorder, played back a little. Shoulda seen the look on his face.

He started getting desperate, begging. Said it would fuck his record up. Couldn't we compromise? He'd do anything. Bingo! Long story short, Larry came to his senses. Promises to be a good little boy. Never touch or say anything naughty again. Said he'd help me out long as I needed. Isn't that nice of him? (She takes the tape out, looks at it) It's amazing what a little tape can do. Just amazing! Wait'll you hear? I gotta play it for you later. S'a real goof.

Men, Marsh. They can drive ya nuts, let me tell you. Who can figure? Who wants too! Besides, no man can make a martini like you. Perfect. Perfect, two olives, straight up. Why don't you bring it over here? Come on. Can't wait. Yum-yum. C'mon, s'been a rough day. I need to unwind.

50's- at the kitchen table. It's been a year since Vernice's son died. His death has left her depressed, manic, and sometimes paranoid. Here she tells her other son, Barry, that her husband is secretly leaving the water overflow in the bathtub every night, flooding the house.

(High energy)

So I'm standing there Barry. Standin' in an inch a water, an it's "Gaslight". Gaslight, you know, that movie with Inga-mar Bergman, where the husband... Well anyway, anyway, ya father says he didn't do a thing. Didn't do a thing he says! Sink musta overflowed by itself. By itself, could ya bust?! Sits over there in his chair. Smug, smiling. Pretendin' like nothin's happened, right?! Readin' his paper. Pretending! But I see him, that son of a bitch. From the corner of my eye, I watch him, watch me, moppin' up. Till he tells me, get this, that I'm "dramatizin" again, okay?! Makin' mountains outta molehills. S'gaslight Barry, I'm tellin' ya! But I'm onto him now. I am. An' he's not gonna get away with it no more. No more Barry! No more! Far as I'm concerned, he can flood the house and float right outta here. I wouldn't even wave good bye. No! To hell with him. To hell with him!

Any age - anywhere. On her way home Sheila's car went out of control on a patch of ice. Here she recalls that terrifying experience.

(at the peak of the story)

My hands, like this, clutched on the wheel. But the car kept swerving out of control. I tried turning, but nothing! And all I could think was, "Why me?! Why now?!" As the car kept skidding. And the other cars passing, honking at me. Beeping like I'm doing it on purpose, right? And your life, your life flashes by. Just like they say. From your first memory on-bing-bing-bing. And I sat there helpless. My God! Was like watching a movie. But me, I was the movie. And my car had a life of it's own; spinning round and round in circles. And me, a piece of puddy strapped in my seat belt. Beyond terror. Beyond beyond! Ready to die, cash in the chips. My death imminent. But then, the strangest thing happened. Wait, wait'll you hear this. I'm sitting there, right? Preparing to die. The car, going round in circles. When for absolutely no reason at all- the car stopped. It just stopped! I kid you not. And there I found myself comfortably parked by the side of the road inside a giant snow drift. Encased, like in a white cocoon. Everything still and quiet except for the sound of the windshield wipers going back and forth, back and forth. And the snow falling. And of course my heart beat pounding all over the front seat. There I was on this quiet night, sitting in my car, not dead. No, not even a scratch. Nothing. Just sitting there with my mouth wide open. But then... I made this sound. Like a whimper. A little whimper. Like a baby in a crib. And the sound opened up more and more. Until I was crying- wailing! Tears pouring. Mascara dripping down my face. Then something inside me whispered, "It's okay. It's over. And you're not dead."

And I said, "Thank you. Thank you God. Thank you! Thank you!!" And I stopped crying. And ya know what I did then? I started to laugh. Yeah! Laugh-laugh-laugh, like a lunatic! Like a crazy woman. But alive. Very alive! Just sitting there in the front seat of my car. Someplace, on some road, God knows where. Inside of this big white cocoon, strapped in my seat belt, looking out the window at the snow. The snow. The snow! (gently) "Hello snow".

20's-40's - a sleazy strip joint. Just as they're ready to go on, Dixie, a perky, happy-go-lucky stripper, tells the new girl the do's and don'ts of the job.

S'a buck, y'know? An' a buck's a buck. They stick it in ya garter, ya bend down, make nice, big smile. An' if ya let 'em flop in their faces- they go crazy! Love it! 'Specially the old guys. I shimmy my titties in their faces- you'd think they'd seen God or somethin'! Their bodies go wild, start spasming. Whatta rush! Cracks me up.

Oh yeah, far as the gropin' goes- what can I say? Look, ya gotta make your own mind on that. My only advice is- a touch can get'cha five. But if ya not into it, then don't. One thing Tony don't like here is if one of his girls is unhappy. Morale's real important. But for me, I'll tell ya, a quick touch, little feel- is lunch an' cigarettes. An' what does it hurt? An' ya make some old guy happy.

Alright, we only dance to the music. S'a twenty minute gig. Music ends, we go. Last thing ya want's to be stranded up there up with nothin' to dance too.

Ya see any guy jerkin' off- look away. If ya stare gets 'em more excited, turns 'em on.

Guess that's it. You take the right side of the stage, I'm on the left. Welcome aboard! Hope I didn't leave anything out. Just play it by ear this first time. Give 'em that smile, an' have a good time. They're here to love you. Ya make some money, no one's hurt. S'not a bad gig. You'll do fine. There's the music. Ready? Ya look great, c'mon. (As she rushes out) Hey, what'd ya say ya name was?

30's-40's - the attic of Maxine and Hanks house. Rough times have fallen on Maxine and her husband Hank. Hank has been out of work for a long time and is feeling the pressure. He has started closing himself off from the rest of the family. Here Maxine tries to convince Hank to come down from the attic and join the rest of the family for dinner.

Look, you're not the only one who's disappointed here Hank. Seems to be the season for it. But you can't just sit here and sulk. We got kids to feed. An' they don't give a rats shit where the money comes from. So just pull yourself together, will ya? Come downstairs. We'll have a good meal, watch some T.V., go to bed early, okay? Hank! Hank, I'm talking to you. Just... Look, maybe tomorrow. Tomorrow's another day. Something'll happen, you'll see. Always does. You'll get a phone call, walk in a right door or something. You'll see. Someone'll say yes, and then you'll feel foolish about this; hiding up here. Hank, will ya turn around please. I don't appreciate your giving me your back. Hank, I'm talking to you! Look, I can't be everything! I don't have the strength anymore. All this is wearing on me just like you. I'm not made a steel, ya know?. I can't keep coming up here every single night begging you to come down and have dinner with us. I can't come up here and get myself drunk like you do every night. Every single night! I got kids to raise. We still got a family, ya know. That's right, keep giving me your back, ga head. See if I care. 'Cause I don't. I really don't care anymore. I don't give a shit. I'm becoming immune. Doesn't hurt anymore. Nothing does! Do you...! I'm talking to you! Are you gonna come downstairs or what?! You want me to tell the kids you're sick again? Is that what you want? Hank, you son of a bitch, I'm talking to you! Hank! Hank!! I'm talking!

30's-40's - Anywhere. Jane has met and dated her share of men over the years, but never met the right one. After giving up for a while, she's decided to start dating again. Here she talks about a man she met the night before, and her renewed hope.

(gently and sincere)

I met a guy last night. He wants to go to the movies with me. I want to do that. His name is Bob. Lives over on West Fifty-First street with his dog, Pete. I haven't been to his place yet, and he hasn't been to mine. I think I like Bob. I really do. Felt so good to be with him last night, walking through the after theater rush. It's funny how when you're with someone you like your concentration is just on them. You don't notice all the people on the street.

I think Bob likes me. I really do. It's a feeling I got while we were walking down Eighth Avenue. The way he looked at me. He walked me home, asked me if he could kiss me good night. I said, "Sure." It was a sweet, gentle kiss. Then we looked at each other for just a bit. He smiled, then I did. I thanked him for walking me home. He said he'd call tomorrow about the movie, smiled again, then left. I just leaned there in the doorway for a while. Happy. Then I went upstairs... alone.

I think... I really think I like Bob, a lot. I hope he like me too.

20's-40's an apartment on the West Side in Manhattan. Elizabeth's sister was recently murdered. Elizabeth has come to New York to sort out her sisters belongings and close out the apartment. While packing some of her sisters things a man sneaks in and attempts to rape her. Here she tells what happened.

(slowly, softly,)

I was... I had a few drinks. Maybe... maybe more than a few, I don't know. I've been... I'm in mourning. My sister Claire died recently. She was killed, here, in this apartment. It's... I was just straightening out some of her things. Having a drink. And this man... from nowhere. I don't know how he got in. Maybe... I don't know, maybe I left the door opened. I don't... He... I was sitting at the table over there. Going through some papers. Bills or something. And he came from behind me. I felt something, turned around. He was just standing there. Looking at me... smiling. A tall man with a gun. Middle of the afternoon. Just... standing there. Then he whispered something. Said if I screamed he'd kill me. Then he came over, started touching me, my shoulder. Was trying to get my blouse off. At first... I just... looked, watched, watched him. Was as if it wasn't me. As if it was someone else. I was like a rag doll being... Was like... I was watching a movie, about someone else. But then...I said, (softly) "No.... No!" My arms started moving. By themselves. All of a sudden. Was like I didn't care. Didn't care if he had a gun. It didn't matter! I started hitting. Swinging my arms! The room started spinning. Going around. I knocked my drink over. I could hear it hit the floor. And then I... went for him. Jumped! Hit! Like an animal! HIT! Looking in his eyes. Hitting! And then, his gun went off- suddenly! And everything stopped! He fell down. The man. He... Everything stopped. And he fell. (a pause) I was just... He tried... I was protecting myself. He was going to... rape me.

30's-60's - on the bed in their bedroom. Here
Georgette tells her husband about a dream she
just had where she dreamt she was the royal
chair to a king.

I dreamt... I dreamt I was a chair, yeah. But not just a
chair, no. A big, thick, cushiony, comfortable, relaxing chair.
Kind you can trust. Bluish-gray, something like that. Soft,
safe. A sit-on-me-anytime, lounging chair. Kind people rely
on. An' in my dream I was brought, well carried, by three or
four slaves to the castle as a gift for the king. And the king-
loved me! Minute he saw me, sat on me, never wanted to get
up. Made me feel so important. Can you imagine, a king
loved me?! Ordered that I be brought to the royal court. I
was gonna replace the throne. Me! Well naturally, in my
dream, I was thrilled. I mean you shoulda seen this place,
the court. Majestic, elegant, chandeliers all over the place.
An' all day long, when court was in session, lords and ladies
standing there, I was the chair under the king. Me! My
cushions carressin' him, my arms under his. If he was tense,
had a difficult decision to make, he'd dig his fingers right into
me; didn't even hurt. An' when he was happy, relaxed, I was
right there, underneath, always supportive.

But then, one night, some guys, the kings enemies I
guess, broke into the castle. Got into the royal chamber.
Started tearin' things up. Stealing. Was terrible. Terrible!
Then they grabbed me. Yeah! Lifted me up. I wanted to
scream, but I'm a chair. Chairs can't scream. They started
tossin' me around. Tossin' me like I'm some cheap piece a
thrift shop furniture. Some second hand knick knack.
Carried me downstairs to a get away wagon parked right
across the moat. Tossed me in, breakin' one of my legs. The
pain! Then they got in and drove off. Little while later when
he discovered I had a broken leg, the guy decided to toss me.
Can you imagine? Threw me out of the wagon. I landed in
some field, middle of nowhere. My back went, cushions all
over the place. I just laid there, as they took off, abandoning
me. Was a dark night, very scary. I just laid there, in pieces,
for hours, looking up. Then... it started to rain. Rained and

rained. All night long. I was getting soaked, drenched. An' all I could think was "My God, mildew. Mildew! I'm gonna rot!"

S'when I woke up. The bed here was soakin' wet. You'd fallen asleep with a beer in your hands again. Bed was drenched. How many times I gotta tell you? Don't bring beer to bed! Now look at this! An' now I'm never gonna find out what happened in my dream. Did the king come? Was I saved? I'll never know. Never!

60's- the bedroom. **For over forty years Edna has kept an important secret from her husband Murray. Her sister Martha once told her that Murray tried to seduce her when they all went up to the country one weekend. Here Edna blurts out the secret she's held onto all those years.**

(Furious)

What?! You wanna know what?!! Okay, alright, I'll tell you' I'll tell you what! How you got her there by the woods. Started touching her- my sister! How she was tryin' to be nice, polite. But you wouldn't stop, would ya?! No! Wouldn't take no for an answer. Kept at it! Couldn't leave her alone, could ya?! Huh, Murray, huh?! You were like some animal, she said. All over her. Until finally... finally, touching wasn't enough, was it? No! You got really disgusting. Opened ya fly, she said. Exposed ya self. Like some pervert! My sister! Why?! Why Murray, huh?! You thought maybe she'd do something with you? An' you said, "Why not? Who'd know?" Like she could care about you! An' then she said she slapped your face good. Good! Good for you! I only wish she'd a ripped your skin off! Then she came runnin' back to the house, tole me about it. Just thank God Herbie didn't see her. He'd a seen her, he'd a ripped you to pieces for sure. For sure he'd a killed you!

30's-40's - A small southern town. Yvonne, a divorcee with a small son, has started dating again. She has finally met the man of her dreams, and they have a date Saturday night. Here she tells her best friend about her hopes for that date.

(very excited)

This Saturday! Saturday night! An' first thing, first thing Saturday morning I am goin' right over to Pearls Beauty Parlor. Gonna do it up lavish. Y'know, curls, whole thing. Then take me straight over to Bolstons for somethin' smart, red, an' too low cut for my own good- thank ya very much! Gonna be positively revealin'!

Then that night when we go out out, I will exude more charm an' grace than ya ever seen before. We'll go somewhere real romantic I bet. Man's got taste. Some candle lit place with a whole lotta atmosphere which I will soak up like some thirsty little sponge s'never had the pleasure. An' I will look only at him, Harriet. Only him! Eyes. His. Mine. Soft music, looks in the dark, hand touchin'. The whole thing!

Harriet, he is the one. The real thing! Matt is a man with a capital M! Right down to his hairy little toes. An' let me tell you, we can certainly use a fixture like that 'round here S'been a long time comin'. But the drought's over. An' Saturday night... Saturday night's gonna be a whole new beginning!

SADIE

30's-50's - in her livingroom. Here Sadie, a full of life divorcee, tells about an exciting encounter she lad with a rabbi.

I looked down at him, smiled, said (sexy), "You can put your key in my door- anytime! Anytime, rabbi."

He blushed, smiled, said I was very forward. Then continued shampooing his beard.

Forward? Well yes, I guess I was. But I wasn't about to make any bones about it. I mean here we'd just been rolling around naked all afternoon on my rubber sheets. Making love in creams and oils. Did he expect formality?! Now?! He was good-very! And I'm sorry I wanted more. Simple as that. Why beat around the bush? Life's too short.

I knew. I did. From that very first look. When he passed me that bagel at the B'nai Brith breakfast. When he asked if I'd like some more lox. Something in his eyes said this man's offering much more than just Nova Scotia. His eyes said sex! Rabbi or not! Threw me completely. Almost dropped my gefilte fish. Yet I managed to stay cordial, polite, continue with the small talk.

Later, all through the meeting, whenever I turned around, he was always looking -right at me. That twinkle in his eyes.

Then after, as everyone was leaving, saying good bye's, he asked if he could walk me home. I said, "Sure". Why not?

And when I saw him in his black coat, black hat, all that hair- so intense. Don't ask! I was turned on. Couldn't wait. So we didn't walk here, no, we flew!

And once we got here, door opened, inside. My God, the rabbi took over! And under all those clothes, there was something I've never known before. Certainly not with any of my ex husbands. Here was someone alive! Vibrant! Virile! Tearing through with such passion. And yet, at the same time- so tender. Willing to teach. Taking me each step of the way. Me, his congregation of one. Following, as he took me to each erotic plateau, each peak. Till finally we both arrived, together, at the same time- the Promised Land! MILK AND HONEY! MY GOD, HE WAS GOOD! DIVINE!

It was a religious experience!

Then after, he was sweet as sugar; gentle as a lamb. A man who took his time, and could be tender- who could ask for more in one lifetime? So the way I see it to go without would almost be sinful. So I offered him my key. What could be wrong? He's a rabbi!

So when he finished blow drying his beard, he stood up, came over to me, gave me a big hug. Said he'd like to see me again. I gave him the key. Said, "Rabbi, my door's always open. Anytime."

Soon after, I became an active member of the synagogue, joined Hadassah, went to temple every day. Saw Sol, my rabbi, often as I could. Last few months we've really gotten to know each other. Gotten very close. Now he uses his key- often. So... the way I see it, maybe, with a little luck, if I play my cards right, who knows? Stranger things have happened, right? Someday could be me and Sol. I mean imagine. I could become... the rabbi's wife.

30's-40's her bed room. As she's finishing
getting dressed, Lou Anne tells about the
dinner she was at the night before. At that
dinner, the daughter of the man she wants to
marry did everything she could to upset her.

I knew it. I jus... knew she'd try to ruin it. Put a wedge
between us. Minute I walked in. The look in her eyes.
Hatred. I knew right then and there the game was over.

I was all dressed up in my nicest dress. Hair done,
perfumed, everything! Spent hours. And there she was, the
little princess. All a what maybe fourteen. Wearin' stained
dungarees, tacky tea shirt, torn socks and no shoes at all.
An' I'll tell ya, if looks could kill... She looked at me like I was
some cheap salesgirl goin' door to door sellin' vacuums. An'
ya jus' knew she wasn't buyin'.

But no matter, I rose to the occasion. Said, "My-my
your daddy didn't do ya justice tellin' me how pretty you
were."

But before I finished my sentence, she said, "You comin'
in or what? We don't need no more flies in here."

I went in. She slamed the door- BANG!

Thank God John came in from the kitchen right away.
Gave me a big hug, said supper'd be ready soon. Said we
should get acquainted. Yeah, right! I wanted to grab him,
apron and all, and run outta there. This was not gonna
work. I just knew it. This girl hated me!

John ran back in the kitchen, leavin' us to do an eyeball
to eyeball in the living room. An' for the next twenty minutes
a so we sat there, hardly sayin' nothin'. You could cut the
air.

Well the meal as you can imagine was tense- very! She
was subtle- but she was good! Knew every trick. From
spilling gravy on me to knocking over my wine- accidentally,
of course. But the highlight was when she knocked the lit
candle on my dress. Was a good thing I didn't go up in
flames. Lucky I'm alive.

Of course I made nothing of it. "Accidents happen dear.
Don't worry." Yeah, sure!

John just thought she was nervous. Excited about meetin' me. Men, what do they know?! He didn't realize she was shootin' from the hip. This girl was well trained. Her mother must have... Well, I kept smiling throughout. My manners, always in check. Constant small talk. "Isn't your dad a divine cook?... This place is so cozy". Like that. Kept it light, lively.

But it was all just a sham. I couldn't wait to escape. Get outta there.

After dinner, when John was driving me home, I couldn't believe how well he felt it went. Naturally, I "yes, deared" him the whole ride. Never mentioned how she kept kicking me under the table, sayin' it was the dog. Really!

But that was last night. Tonight's gonna be a whole different kettle a fish. I'm going back. Us girls gonna talk. He'll be at work. She's there doing her home work. Tonight it's gonna be a girl to girl and the etiquette will be dropped! (She puts her jacket on) Tonight little princess some lessons will be learned. Tonight I will be... myself.

40's- 60's - a waiting room. Seeing her son stoned on drugs was a harrowing experience for Sydelle. Here she recalls that night to a woman she's just met.

He'd fallen down. Knocked over the table. Couldn't get up. Glass all over the place. His pants, soakin' wet from peein' in em. Saliva drippin' from his mouth. Terrible! An' he's pretendin' nothin's wrong, right? My first impulse, I'll tell ya, I wanted to kill him; beat him up right there. But I just stood there in shock. Couldn't believe my eyes. How come I never knew?! How come?! I looked at him down there like he's some disease crawling around on my kitchen floor. S'like all of a sudden he's not your kid. S'like he's some drugged out stranger, pathetically pretendin' nothin's wrong. Pretendin it's okay to be crawlin' around on broken glass at three in the mornin'.

"What'sa matta' ma?", he says. "What'cha lookin' at? What, ma? What?! What's wrong?!"

An' all you can think is, my God, s'my kid. S'my son! Sixteen, just sixteen! Gotta whole life ahead a him. Look at him! What I do wrong? Who's fault...?! How'd this...?! How come I never knew?!! An' ya heart breaks. I know. I know it does. Breaks in half. You wanna cry - but'cha can't. You wanna help him, sure- but'cha wanna kill him too. At the same time! You're torn apart. How could this happen? How could he do this?! How?!!

But... in the end, he's your son. Flesh and blood. So you help him up, wipe him off, wash him, put him to bed.

An' I don't know about 'chu, but for me- for me, was the longest night a my life. I prayed, cried, carried on. Never thought I'd get through it. But I did. Next day, I told him, said, "You go for help, you understand?! You go, or I call the cops! No two ways about it! I'm not havin' no drug addict here! Not here! Not under my roof! Never!"

So he went, thank God. I went with him to make sure. First thing next morning. Started treatment, worked hard. For a long time. Did a three hundred and sixty degree turn with his life. Wasn't easy. I'm not sayin' it was. But we all helped. The whole family. One day at a time. A real team effort.

Well, that was 'bout five years ago. Lotta water under the bridge. Things change. Now... now, he's a whole different person. Now he helps- others. Runs this clinic- my son. My son! I just came up here to have lunch with him. He's in there. Oh, he's with your boy? Well then don't worry miss. Your son's in good hands. My boy's been there. Been through it. You're lucky. Lucky ya caught it in time. It's a disease, drugs . A terrible disease. Kills 'em. Destroys their minds. But your son's gonna be alright. 'Cause he's there with my boy. And my son won't let him down, no matter what.

20's-30's - Anywhere. Celia's been a runaway, a drifter, since she was fifteen. Here, she tells about the day she tried to get her belongings from an apartment of two men she was staying with. One of the men refused to let her take her stuff. Here is how she handled it.

Meetin' Marty that day was a big mistake. Big one! Absolutely! I told him, I said I wanted my stuff, I was leavin'. But he said, "No way. No one's takin' nothin' outta here without Ciggys okay. Go find Ciggy", he said. "Maybe he's down the corner."

I said, "Marty, Marty, don't fuck with me. C'mon, I'm in a hurry. I can't wait. Gotta ride outside. Some guy I met. We're goin' to Florida."

"No.", he kept sayin', "No! No!"

I said, "Marty, I gotta go. I need my shit."

But he stood there, son of a bitch. Front of the bedroom door. Wouldn't let me in.

"Nobody gets nothin' from here without Ciggys' okay. You know that."

"Marty, c'mon. You, Ciggy, you guys been great. Really. We had a lotta good times. Lotta laughs. I'll never forget ya's. But I met a guy. And he wants to take me to Florida. Florida, Marty. Florida!- where it's clean an' warm. An' there's sunshine all the time. An' not you or nobody else is gonna fuck it up. I'm gonna go!"

But he stood there, the bastard. Said, "Nobody takes nothin' without Ciggy. I only listen to him."

So you see I had no choice. None. He forced me. I pulled out my piece, held it to his head.

"You wanna be that way?! You wanna be that way?!! Ga head, be a prick," I said. "Ga head, you always are. Even Ciggy says so. But I'm gonna Florida, and you're not gonna stop me."

See Marty don't really know me. He don't know 'bout my life. Don't know about all the guys that have stood in front a me since I was fuckin' fifteen years old. Guys that wouldn't let me go. Made me do what they wanted, when they wanted it. So when I gotta gun- when I'm holdin', nobody tells me what or what not to do anymore. An' I think Marty got that clear 'cause he moved away from the door; let me get my stuff.

"Ciggy'll be angry", he said. "Ciggy'll be real pissed."

I packed up. Never took my eyes or the piece off a Marty. He watched me like a fuckin' hawk. 'An when it was time to go Marty made his one big mistake. He tried to stop me. He shouldn'ta. We fought and the gun went off. One shot. One hit to the head, and Marty fell down. I couldn't fuckin' believe it. What an asshole! I looked down at him for a minute, then I split. Ran. Ran real fast. Ran down the stairs. Got outside, into the car where Ciggy was waitin' for me.

"How'd it go?", he said.

I lied. Told him it went fine. Said yeah, Marty was pissed, but I knew someday he'd understand. He just needed time. Maybe they could be friends again some day. Then I kissed Ciggy. Put my arms around him, held him real close. He smelled so good. We both looked back for a minute, then he started the car. Then me 'an Ciggy, we left, went to Florida.